W0259475

53SP 22
October 2015

ISBN no. 978-0-9897393-5-1
Library of Congress Control no. 2015937855

53rdstatepress.org

First page image by Amanda Villalobos

Corrected edition with expanded notes.

LET US NOW PRAISE SUSAN SONTAG

SIBYL KEMPSON

WITH MUSIC BY ASHLEY TURBA

53RD STATE PRESS
BROOKLYN, NEW YORK

"The root is so rotten. The whole values system is so based on everyone being brainwashed to believe that you have to fucking compete with everyone else and that there isn't enough to go around so just get used to it some people are poor and some people suffer and some people don't and it's all the way it works and it's arrogant and arrogant and pessimistic to talk about poverty. Just say inequality, call it unequal and unfair and that's a part of life and it's not oppression it's just not really that nice but oh my it is that nice when the church gives out all the turkeys. Give away the turkeys and give away more turkeys and don't talk about it. Just give them away."

— Lee Sunday Evans, THE BIG FIX

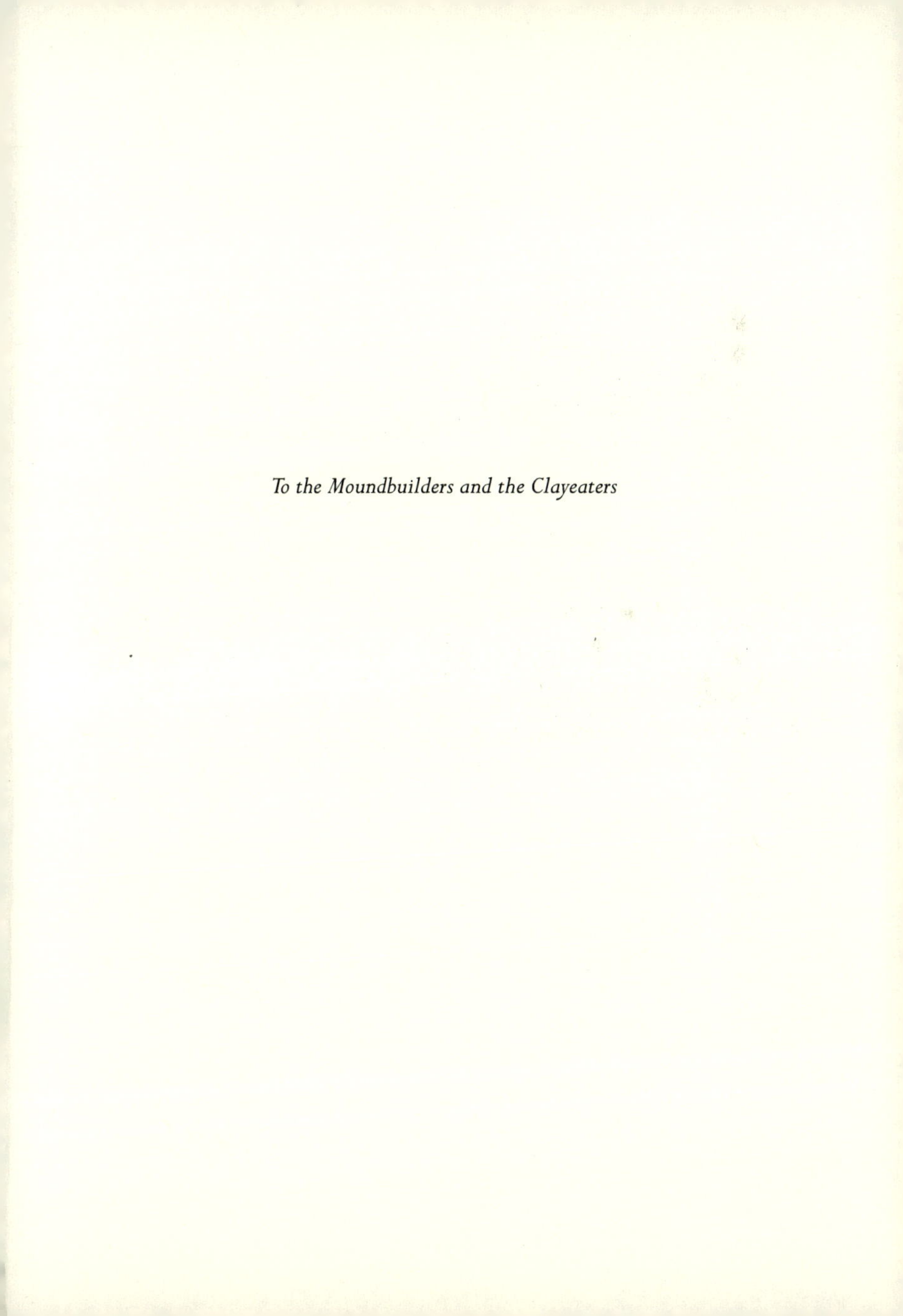

To the Moundbuilders and the Clayeaters

Cast for the New York premiere
Abrons Arts Center, April 2015

Tory	Eleanor Hutchins
Steve	Rolls Andre
Linda	Tanya Selvaratnam
Sarah	Sarah Willis
Andrew	Becca Blackwell
Jay	Robert M. Johanson
Ben	Gavin Price
Jean Ann	Amanda Villalobos
Susan Sontag	Tanya Selvaratnam, Sibyl Kempson
Adapa	Tavish Miller
Band	Johnny Gasper, Gavin Price, Ellery Royston

Stage Manager	Eryk Aughenbaugh
Dramaturgy	Jody McAuliffe, Eryk Aughenbaugh
Choreography	David Neumann
Set & Costumes	Suzanne Bocanegra
Music Director	Gavin Price
Sound Design	Ellery Royston
Lighting	Sarah Lurie
Construction	Brendan Regimbal, Laurena Allan, Jake Denney
Understudy	Tavish Miller
Producer	Meredith Boggia

FOREWORD

When I first talked to Sibyl Kempson about her new play, *Let Us Now Praise Susan Sontag*, she told me that her source materials were James Agee's *Let Us Now Praise Famous Men* and *Land and Life* by Carl Sauer. As luck would have it, I had recently finished a course on ethics in documentary practice at the Center for Documentary Studies at Duke University. I recommended to Kempson an article that had made a powerful impression on me, "The Most Famous Story We Never Told," in which the shamed and wronged children of white sharecroppers – photographed and documented during the Depression by Agee and Walker Evans – revisit with bitter resentment the way in which their families were represented in Agee's florid prose and Evans' striking photographs. The *Fortune* magazine author David Whitford notes that the pictures do not portray the three families as "you or I would wish to be seen," that is, scrubbed, combed, clean, and smoothed for the camera.

Kempson's creative process involves doing a lot of reading and then writing what she calls "irrational responses" to what she's been reading: spontaneous and intellectually unmediated reactions. She begins working with actors and writes in response to what they are doing, and broadens the field of research in an intuitive way that includes the associations of the performers and other collaborators. She eventually emerges from what she calls the "brambles" to brilliant lucidity. I was fortunate to participate in this associative exchange with her. Engaging with such disparate texts as Stephen Eisenman's *The Abu Ghraib Effect*, Odilon Redon's *To Myself: Notes on Life, Art, and Artists*, and Roland Barthes' *Camera Lucida*, Kempson collides abject conditions of poverty against ideas about high art, aesthetics, and ethics. Mix in *The New American Machinists Handbook* and the wild and crazy Youtube Yosemitebear Mountain Double Rainbow, and you are plunged with hilarity and insight directly into the Kempsonian universe.

On the cotton fields of northern Alabama, site of Stone Age and Paleo-Indian history, she sets about interrogating our perceptions of the civilized in relation to ideas of the barbaric, the sacred, and the true. In the ordinary lives and seemingly ordinary language of her version of the Cotton Tenants, Kempson contacts the signals and patterns of a deeper ontological order that she has the unique penetrating vision to perceive. In imaginative and playful theatrical terms, she tracks the Assyrian seals housed at the Morgan Library – through the Paleo-Indian culture of semi-nomadic hunter-foragers and the lost civilization of mound builders, through Evans' harsh, plain photographs – directly to Susan Sontag herself, back from the dead to invite us to perceive new meanings, to know differently what we see.

The idea that photography heightens aesthetic awareness, but anesthetizes ethical response, is a driving force inside the play. In his luminous text, *Camera Lucida*, Roland Barthes describes the "punctum" of a photograph – a detail that pricks us. Barthes analyzes a photograph of a condemned man. (What are these cotton tenants if not condemned?) The prick is our discovery of the equivalence of "this will be" and "this has been." Like psychotic patients, we shudder over a catastrophe that has already occurred. For Barthes, "whether or not the subject is already dead, every photograph is this catastrophe." The "poof" moments – live photographs punctuating the play – are punctums: actors freeze and are immortalized.

Kempson's sharp interrogation of these "beautiful" photographs coincides with a new historical understanding of the dependent relationship among the production of cotton, slavery, sharecropping, and the growth of capitalism in this country. She reads the signs surrounding us and creates a new myth, which is her play: *Let Us Now Praise Susan Sontag*. For her, our dearest hope is in the land. Contact with the land ignites a vision of possibility, of ringing cedars, of ascendance, of blessing. The deep connection to the past is the path to progress.

Sibyl Kempson, like Joseph Conrad, "speaks to our capacity for delight and wonder, to the sense of mystery surrounding our lives; to our sense of pity, and beauty, and pain; to the latent feeling of fellowship with all creation – and to the subtle but invincible conviction of solidarity that knits together the loneliness of innumerable hearts, to the solidarity in dreams, in joy, in sorrow, in aspirations, in illusions, in hope, in fear, which binds men to each other, which binds together all humanity – the dead to the living and the living to the unborn."

— Jody McAuliffe, 2015

NOTES TO THE READER

Sibyl's shows are exactly the kind of challenge I enjoy as a performer: getting entangled in scenarios and speech that don't play into convention or play to be liked. In her inimitable, fantastical, yet grounded style, Sibyl captures her characters through poetry from another planet that makes perfect sense if you pay attention to it and give in to it. Memorizing her words is like learning a new language. As performers, we had to embrace the logic of the lines and not put too much on top of them, convey the intricacies of the story clearly to the audience, and be rigorous in drilling our lines and inhabiting our characters. We were members of a family, and it was especially important that we support each other, that we listen to each other.

—Tanya Selvaratnam

These characters that Sibyl wrote – they are each carrying a ton of tonnage. They are layered up, and I thought they each need to carry their stuff, all the time – like a traveling salesman, like a peddler.

First I thought of Eugene Atget's photos of peddlers from late 19th-century Paris. Photographed by Atget in a simple and noble way, they were walking stores, a scrappy and hard living group. Those photographs estheticize poverty, the beauty that you can see in rags and old shacks, especially when you aren't the ones living in them. They tapped into the same issues that that Sibyl grapples with, in the Walker Evans photos that the Susan Sontag character deals with in the play.

But these Parisian peddlers were too real for me. I realized I needed something to start with that had more artifice, that was estheticized even more. Something more pretend.

I thought of a doll I saw once in England, in the flea market on Portobello Road. It was a peddler doll – a doll about 15 inches high, with lots of miniaturized bits and bobs hanging off her belt and apron and piled on a tray she carried like a cigarette girl. She was charming. Peddler dolls were made in England from the 16th to the 19th century, for rich ladies to collect and admire. They were not to be played with.

Ok, filter the depression-era Walker Evans photos through the old English peddler dolls. That seemed perfect and I went from there.

— Suzanne Bocanegra

Each of the songs in this play is an ecstatic release, allowing the characters to freely express themselves: Steve can really let us know about the machines he's been thinking about, and Andrew can express his love in his uniquely stilted way. We approached each piece of the stylistically ranging music as a process of discovery, experimenting with harmonies, sometimes writing parts for new instruments, or tweaking a rhythm until it really flowed. The songs were written with this incarnation of the band in mind, but any ragtag group of musicians should feel free to swap out instruments and add their own flourishes, as we did.

— Ellery Royston

I find it impossible to sit still through a Sibyl Kempson play, but only because the magnitude so completely envelops that to not move about and participate feels like sleeping through the day. Rather than the classic arrangement of performer-audience partition, the energy her work inspires is closer to the tradition of haunted houses and backyard history plays, but also street social-protest theater. In *Let Us Now Praise Susan Sontag*, a play ostensibly concerned with the lack of subject self-determination in poetic journalism, the audience is rendered into the position of the second person, empowered with full access to not only the physical world but also the complex panorama initiated by Tory's visions, a gateway into the the family's arcane and dwindling nonmaterial cultural essence. It's fine to dwell on the minutia or to let yourself be washed over in a torrent of images; Kempson's theater is a landscape and there's much to see and hear.

— Eryk Aughenbaugh

Let Us Now Praise Susan Sontag

Characters

(In order of appearance)

Tory, a cotton tenant farmer

Steve, her brother-in-law

Linda, older sister of Tory, wife of Steve

Sarah, the baby of the family, except for the baby

Andrew, Tory's husband

Jay, a journalistic photographer from the Big City

Ben, a journalistic writer from the Big City

Jean Ann, known as JAGSTAR in her showbiz career, sister to Tory

Susan Sontag, reputed radical intellectual

Adapa, a Bird-Fish-Carp-Man-Eagle, ancient Mesopotamian sage

Note: When a double slash (//) appears in the text, it is an indication that the next spoken line overlaps the present one, beginning at the slash mark.

Preamble, Verses, Introductions

Tory is the first to address us, the strangers who have come onto the property and have asked to please speak to and take photographs of them. She steps out gingerly and takes a seat.

EVERYBODY: POOF.

TORY: The second one is a memory I have,
but of something that never happened to me.
Of rowing or paddling? A boat? Through reeds –
and no, it's not Moses or something,
not really from that part of the world,
I don't THINK. I think it's HERE, even.
But I do not know.
No.
But I'm paddling.
I come to the bank of it, of the water.
A lot of brush growing. Only if you're an animal
can you get through it,
or if you can hack your way through it like a white man,
doing all the conquering.
Or, you could be an animal instead and get through it that way.
You're noplace and then suddenly you are in a place.
This never happened to me. And yet at the same time
I remember it! … and I get there, or here? and it's all marble,
and it's crumbling down.
It's a huge monument,

of some kind, and with big pieces and it's like.

Really intimidating.

BIG pieces.

And two things happened to me there.

#1.) I came to know God.

#2.) I came to no god.

This is in the brush, in the woods. And there are people living around there.

Do they? Does anyone even know these big pieces are here? What is this? An old busted up tub machine of some kind. The ruins of it.

Steve pokes his head out the window-hole of the house to add some vaudeville to the scene.

STEVE: Whaddya think my name is Fink and I press pants for nothing! Whaddya think my name is Fink and I press pants for nothing!

TORY: Even the force that made these, which was human or very close to human but without the sort of like "I'm the best and you owe me so what's for lunch?" kind of attitude. Look, not that you all are like that – taking what you can get and selling it. Not all of you. Some of you seem to understand when to get down on your knees and when to stand up and lend a hand. So EVERYBODY RELAX.

That force that made this place, I'm talking about this circle of pillars and steps that was still standing in a lot of ways but mostly just a pile of rubble that was really something. And something really happened there. To me. Although this did not ever happen to me. And I remember it.

First there are some nice looking horned animals grazing. Like maybe big sheep? Or cows. Both? Everything is fine and the boundaries are clear between what land is for this and what land is for that, and who is in charge of who. Until these FELINES show up – ! Huge FELINES who are HUNGRY! And they are like jumping on the sheep or the cows and the men are like, "Hey! NO." And suddenly ONE PARTICULAR guy, who is wearing a <u>kilt</u> shows up with a sword and fights them. He wins, he always wins, but whereas we would see that as the end of the story it's like NO. But that's all we know. Kilt-wearing bearded hero fights against big cats attacking horned animals grazing. It stands for something else, a whole nother level of meaning, but we don't know what.

I was never there. I remember being there. And looking at all this stuff. It was all really beautiful.

The horns on those big beasts were hard to make out as horns, because it was so worn away in the marble. It COULD ... have been bunny ears ...

Linda enters.

LINDA: Tory. That's enough. Time to get inside. You can't just stand out there and talk about that kind of stuff.

Tory slumps off into the house.

EVERYBODY: POOF.

LINDA: *(Re: visitors.)* Kill the cat. There's comp'ny comin. *(Then, to visitors, in confidence.)* All right. I would care to discuss something to you some 'back-ground information.' It's not about Tory's half-sister Jean Ann who ran off, married, ran off and don't live here anymore. I think it's about Sarah, the baby of the family, except for the baby. It happened right before she grew up. She went into the town one day to talk to a doctor about Steve, her father. Again. And when she was crossing the street to join Tory who was selling eggs and butter and go on the way home she got hit by a lady-of-position's cart and she had to turn right around and go back into the doctor office to pay for a surgery to mend it. It's hard to remember who exactly this all happened to. So, even though shortly thereafter she came down with a terrible brain infection, in compensation the lady sent her a whole full outfit of brand new clothes in a box and all wrapped up in fine tissue paper which we kept and still keep in the corner dresser drawer with the twine, and use again, to wrap other things on special occasions. A whole full outfit. Petticoats and a skirt over it and a peplum and pintucks and embroidery all around showing a tender scene, // and ribbons sewn in and a matching hairband, all of it of satin, pink satin, with frills and a matching little jacket and shoes of bright shiny patent leather.

SARAH: Tender scene concealing an ugly truth.

Tory looks at her out the window, recognizes and remembers the tale Linda is telling. Goes to gather up the different remaining pieces of the outfit which are hanging from the nails where they hang inside the house. Linda continues.

LINDA: And once she was up and about again she wore it once or twice the whole outfit. She was really dazzling but it was too much for around here and people laughed at her behind her back, or worse – accused her of having stole it, also behind her back. It looked ridiculous – especially working out in the fields TENANT FARMERS DO NOT PLOW IN SWALLOWTAILS as they say, and she wore it every day for a while but then just wore pieces of it matched up to try and sort of dress the shabbier clothes up a little. *(Ad lib: examples of what she put with what.)*

Tory comes out of the house with what is left of the outfit, pieced back together in its former order. She either pins it to her own person, or else she carries it, or drapes it over a chair and carries the chair, or maybe puts it on Sarah and brings or carries Sarah out to show everyone. And if she does that, we get the impression that it's not the first time that's happened and that Sarah hates this outfit and the whole narrative halo emanating from it.

TORY: And then there's this embroidered scene embroidered on it, this here blue sun inside a circle and a family standing by a stream – in the stream? you can't tell anymore and we like to argue about it on Sundays. And a man with a coat and tails and the tails are so long they look like a fish tail...

SARAH: Or swallowtails? Ha.

TORY: I always said it's a fish-eagle-man. But nobody wants to hear that.

LINDA: And there used to be a grass lawn on it made out of real green ribbon. But it got all chewed apart.

SARAH: And see how he's holding his arms like so, as if to to communicate something to the young townslady standing near the little river. And her family behind her...

TORY: Jean Ann used to profess to know what he was telling them. Her.

SARAH: Some kind of love story.

TORY: A different reflection. Heh.

EVERYBODY: POOF.

LINDA: Then after a while the things the rich lady had given her – began to fade and split and fray. So you couldn't remember their former splendor. Their half-life splendor was all they still contained, for the shine of satin takes a while to completely die away.

SARAH: Long half-life-shelf-life.

LINDA: Then when it started to fray and tear that's when we started in with patches from flour sacks, fertilizer sacks, and feed sacks. So it makes a mosaic sort now, dudn't it. Not bad.

SARAH: And now it fits <u>me</u>. So we keep it around. Even though Jean Ann is long gone someplace in the outer world.
Huh. Half-truth.

TORY: Well, it's the story of a lot of these clothes, actually. They were all pretty much fresh at one time. But they all fade and fray and smell sour once they learn what kind of work they'll be doing from now until the end of time.

Linda looks at Steve.

LINDA: Were you hearing her? Did you hear what she was saying? Before?

STEVE: Not really.

LINDA: Did you participate?

STEVE: Should we tell the way we met?

LINDA: Yes, but just a minute. Let me finish. When she starts doing that I don't feel safe. I start wondering how the house will be kept if I get sick, or something happens and I can't do it. Barely gets kept now. Look at this place. And I'll be lying there and I'm too sick or too old to clean everything the way it ought, and then I just have to lie there, and watch things get – And then lay in it? Stains down my front?

STEVE: It's already like that.

LINDA: Worse than now

STEVE: Um.

LINDA: She's going to end up kicked out of the community, and then not being protected by anyone. And do you know what happens then? That's what's going to end up happening.

Linda goes back into the house, slamming the torn screen door.

Steve waits a moment.

STEVE: I guess it's the daughters who are supposed to – you're supposed to teach them in such a way that they'll be ok with taking over the upkeep once you can't do it anymore. They're trying to decide whether it's a daughter situation or not. I don't think it is. It looks more to me like an older sister trying to turn it into a daughter situation.

Do you like if I tell you about what the relationships are? Even if it's not true it gives you something to go on? If you need it? Or can I tell you about the machines I'm thinking about? Is that ok, if I talk about that for a little while?

I get bored with relationships and personal situations. Personally.

Linda comes back out, putting something different in place about her appearance. Likely something about her hair. When she's finished, she takes Steve by the hand.

LINDA: He lived down on the other, the West, end. Let's see, and I was active in the church and the church bazaars. They were having a fair in the basement and I told them my thing would be that I set up a fortune teller's tent.

Steve puts an arm around.

STEVE: And she was really good at telling those fortunes.

LINDA: There was a practical joke getting played and they were going to shut out all the lights so that all the boys could kiss their sweethearts.

STEVE: And they asked me, since I didn't have a sweetheart, if I would blow out the candle in Linda's tent, since that would be the only light that would give anything away.

LINDA: He said he would. Those boys didn't know he was already madly in love with me.

STEVE: Even though she was engaged to someone else.

LINDA: *(Shutting him up.)* Ehnt! And he was a widower to a wealthy landowner's daughter!

STEVE: Appendicitis. But I don't like being told if I want something that I can't have it.

LINDA: Eh, Steve –

STEVE: Or at least that time I didn't.

LINDA: Ahem.

STEVE: So when she went off to ______, it was with a bundle of daguerreotypes I went and had taken of myself in a dozen or so lovelorn attitudes. And I just let those photos go to work on her. Didn't I, Linda.

LINDA: Ahem. Now we're here.

Silence.

SARAH: Is that true?

Pause.

TORY: No.

LINDA: It is too true. You wouldn't remember. You weren't alive. Shoot. I wasn't alive yet either.

SARAH: And wasn't there a fire? Didn't the whole // church burn // down?

LINDA: Shh.

TORY: Yeah.

SARAH: I remember hearing.

TORY: That part is true. That their forbidden love burned a whole church down.

Linda looks at Tory.

TORY: *(To Linda.)* And NOW. We're here.

SARAH: Ahoo.

EVERYBODY: POOF.

SARAH: So a coupla fellas show up on a one Sunday, to have a look at the place, they say. They've got a camera, they've got writing utensils and dark hair and clean clothes. They're strangers. They stroll up and they say …

STEVE: *(Yelling.)* Whaddya think my name is Fink and I press pants for nothing!

Furniture.

SARAH: I go: hey, what's up we're not Swedish and we're not Norwegians. This ain't the prairie and this ain't Little House Up a Prairie. We're not lookin at the future, we're not dusting the furniture, we're not lookin in the mirror. We're not living in a neat row of a dozen gaily painted farmhouses that spell out the word success if you look at it from a bird with a massive wingspan flying overhead at dawn. We're not doing literature. No big red barns here. We didn't settle this land. And so how do we live. I'll tell you: March to June, while cotton is cultivated: six to ten dollars a month rations money, and that's a gamble. July to late August, while cotton is making: however we can. Late August to October or early November: on six dollars a bale more or less while cotton is picking and ginning from our two-thirds share of the cottonseed and three-fourths of the corn, minus what we owe the landlord on two-thirds and three-fourths the price of fertilizer, plus interest, and plus interest on the rations money. That's eight percent interest, mister. And not a penny do we see til the first bale is ginned. Until March, we live however we can, and no help from anybody. So a lot of times we end up in debt with no work and nothing to eat all winter. And don't take ill. In our group. Land doesn't mean freedom *(music)* or even openness. You look like you got a chip on your shoulder. *(Tempo increase.)* You're looking around here like you just stumbled on a goldmine. Whatta ye Comm'nist? Well, we here are having a tough day. We're all real, real tired. Don't look around here like that. Quit it! Yuck.

SONG: NO LITTLE HOUSE ON SOME PRAIRIE

I go: Hey! Hey! Hey!
This ain't no prairie
No little house on some prairie
We're not lookin in the future
Not lookin in the mirror
Not dustin any furniture

This ain't no prairie
No little house on some prairie
We didn't settle this land
But we work it with our own hands
You look around where you stand
It's real rough, it's been tough a-a-anndd
I go: Hey! Hey! Hey!
This ain't no prairie
No little house up some prairie

But what I really said was.

Nothing.

They spoke first.

She waits for them to speak. It takes a long time.

From the window-hole Tory says.

TORY: Hello.

A couple of photographs are snapped.

JAY: Click.

SARAH: They were wearing yellow shoes. I remember staring at them. He was. The one fella. I'm staring at their feet. I'm not used to strangers.

JAY: Click. Snap! Shoot.

My God. How can human beings survive in a place like this way.

Snap. Shoot.

Look, they do not even have shoes to put on their feet. Only dirty bandages.

Snap. Shoot.

ANDREW: Well that's just what we have.

Tory is my wife and Sarah is the baby of the family. Except for the baby.

I walk four miles to my workplace and arrive just after dawn.

STEVE: Yeah. And Linda is my wife and we own this land and these people rent it from us.

It's our risk. We're the ones absorbing the risk. Everyone else just lives off of us.

LINDA: Steve, stop lying. We don't own anything. Not even a mule anymore. //You a-hole.

Steve used to be married to the daughter of one of the land-owners. //That's where he learned that filthy talk like that.

STEVE: He-ey!

TORY: That's not true either.

BEN: Well, we're here from *Daily Business Weekly* – the magazine? to study and report on you guys. On what you do, on your end of the spectrum. We'll need to stay with you here at the house so we can really get an idea of what to report.

Don't worry chuckle chuckle – we really won't be much trouble.

JAY: Linda. You don't remember me?

Linda steps down away from Steve to look at Jay for a minute.

LINDA: No. Should I?

She looks again for another minute. He steps out from behind his camera and makes a gesture where it is like he is examining her eye.

STEVE: What the hell is *that* supposed to mean?

LINDA: Oh, yeah. Now I remember.

Steve steps back up and Linda puts his arm back around her.

LINDA: *(Cont'd.)* Well, this is different. This is a totally different situation.

JAY: But what about your feelings? Are they any different? Because in the end, that is what is matters most.

LINDA: I SAID I'M WITH STEVE NOW!

JAY: Oh, hm? I must have missed out. I did not hear you say so.

Linda looks at Ben now.

LINDA: You look familiar to me too.

Ben shrugs, keeping his shoulders pinned up to his ears until Linda looks away.

LINDA: Oh, God I don't know what to do! I'm too tired!

SONG: A SONG OF TRYING TO REMEMBER

You were my son
Or I was in Las Vegas
We did we enjoy
The life of pretty danger
I just can't cannot
I cannot remember
Don't piss me off
I don't want to go deeper

This is a song of trying to remember

Day One of pain
Exquisite pain without you
I lay face down
Under the weeping willow
Good-bye, Good-bye
I definitely already told you
Why did you have to
Show up there in person.
Needless to say
I was over-joyed to see you

This is a song of trying to remember
Though
I only remember
The first two rifle shots

This is a song of trying to remember
Good-bye, good-bye
I definitely already told you
This is a song of trying to remember

Inductions

BEN: *(To Sarah.)* Young lady, you're a very young lady: adolescent daughter. Raised on nothing but chicken meat and two to three cups of black coffee every meal. // You'll see me relating to you with respect. Don't worry. We're going to have a lot of long talks. *(Soothingly.)* And I'm going to write everything down. And you'll be amazed by my writing skills someday.

TORY: It's all she'll eat!

He opens up a typewriter with a flourish that demonstrates his fabulous writing skills. Tory looks on with a certain amount of silent suspicion and hostility.

JAY: If she can even learn to read anything around here. Good Christ. Hold still, if you please.

SARAH: POOF!

Strains of the song "Yellow Shoes" are heard. Sarah speaks over them.

SARAH: Aperture. I learned about aperture, though we didn't get to ask a lot of questions and I'm too tired to ask questions, not used to strangers. Because I mostly only. You know? I am still a child at this time.

JAY: Pretty starving child do not smile.
You will ruin my picture.

Listen to the click, or clunk, of equipment
You know cameras will not always be made from wooden.
Done from the wood.
We must enjoy these kind of mechanics while we can.

Tory enters.

TORY: The big stones are heavy and difficult,

BEN: Ugh – are you <u>alright</u>?

TORY: put by beings who were insisted on something.

BEN: My God, you certainly must have been a looker. // In the days of – of your – ?

TORY: Something beyond just survival.

BEN: But how old are you even? // I can't tell.

JAY: It is impossible to tell.

BEN: I can't tell by looking at your poor shriveled face, your corn-rotted teeth or your swollen, knotty hands. The stoop of your back. No. I can't tell by looking at the skin that isn't covered, chuckle chuckle. // Don't worry. Jay won't take any "Nudes."

TORY: Intimidating stone structures of my dim dreams. Visitation of Giants, // of Sons of God. Eagle Fish Men With Messages From the Horizon.

SARAH: GIANTS!

BEN: But I can just try to describe it – you – your – skin –

TORY: If you could imagine them, you'd be intimidated too, bud.

BEN: – as well as my powers will let me *(another 'writing' flourish),* so rough and drained of life.

TORY: Worshipper Approaching Enthroned Water God and Two-Faced // High Official in a Sanctuary? Huh?
Guarded by Nude Bearded Heroes Grasping Gateposts? How 'bout it. Lion-Headed Eagles Attacking Fallen God? Huh?
Y'know?
Click.

SARAH: TWO-FACE!!

Ben waits for her to finish and move on to something else, perplexed and uninterested.

SARAH: *(To Jay.)* Seated Man With Unshaved Neck Among Needy Five-Pointed Leaves with Bolls on Thin Stalks. Click.

TORY: Ours are a short, difficult timespan of being alive, but we hardly know the difference // and we put only the necessary shelter and to live.

BEN: *(Now scribbling everything Tory's saying into a notebook.)* Yuh-huh … Uh-huh …

TORY: Beds, something of the roof still over our heads. // Our sacred combinations of thoughts. We keep those.

BEN: Uh-huh … Mm. Uh-huh …

SARAH: *(To Jay.)* Sleepy Mule Head With Shorn Bridle With Chains. Click. Snap.

TORY: The one biggest blessing, and which holds us together and keeps us going. // Is clean, cold water. And that is God's grace that lets us have it for our faces upon waking up more exhausted than when we lay down, and it is again God's grace that lets us wash our tired hot feet with it at the end of the wrenching day.

BEN: Uh-huh … Nuh-huh … Uh-huhn.

TORY: Now, as twilight approaches, I try to hang on. I can never stay awake at night. // It's the only time when the time passes slowly.

BEN: Oh I can! That's when I WRITE! *(A flourish.)*

TORY: And now the darkness of another night has gathered, what little time is left I use to love the earth with my mind.// The dirt, the dust, the light coming up through the cracks in the floor – we leave everything there. Let me remember in the time that is left in this day. To send love there with my mind.

SARAH: Yeaaaah!

BEN: And yeah. And so. I've seen you washing your feet at night in a bucket and then taking that dirty foot water out to the plants and watering them with it. What's up with that.

SARAH: The plants that we can eat. It's a form of medicine. That's how we give them our information. Once they have that, they know what to do.

JAY: And then what you eat them?

BEN: Isn't that against the law?

LINDA: That's how we get through the winter, son. We found that if we eat them we don't get as sick. Our babies don't die as many.

TORY AND LINDA: POOF.

TORY: And if Each Day is a Lifetime, and Each Lifetime is a Day. Only so much strength per person, per day, per lifetime. Me? Believe me, bro, I don't want to be such a mess like this! Barefoot even on Sundays...

LINDA: That lady who bought the outfit for Jean Ann – When you see her she is always clean and neat and fresh. And has had ample rest. People hanging up her things for her and totally ironing all her sheets and clean hankies – with starch!

TORY: How d'you know?

LINDA: Bedpan and the chamberpot – She doesn't even have to go outside. No hole in <u>her</u> porch, mister. They take it all outside <u>for</u> her. Bowl and pitcher'll scrubbed and rinsed and filled with water from a well! She can sit nice and watch the rain from a window.

TORY: And anyway we've got our own way of water…

We work all day, and the little babies and children, they need care, just the most basic care.
If they make it,
when they get big enough to work,
if they don't die,

LINDA: Of the seven children we have lost, one lived to be four –

TORY: *(Cont'd.)* and if we have the five dollars
or else which to pay the granny-woman for delivery, and don't have to pay her with the baby itself and can keep them, it pays off.

LINDA: It's true you can't rightly expect a child to bring in much til they're 5 or 6. But you can't learn em too young …

Andrew enters.

ANDREW: I'm seeing the way these guys are looking around here. I'm looking down the barrel of this thing you're pointing at me. You're a human, and I'm a human. But this thing separates us. It's hot out here, we're both here sweating. All of us are. You didn't work out in those fields all day like I did,

but you're not out on the cool veranda at the Peabody Hotel drinkin a mint julep either. You're here with us. You shared with us what we had to eat tonight. Then you go and put that thing, and point it at me. Aim it at me. Shoot. Take. I'm looking down the barrel – I see further ahead. They got em hangin from trees – men and women – and men & women standin in front of em. Pillars of the Community. Coal miners on the porch, just like ours. Take one. Dead girlchild – and a big group of em like you – climbin over each other, like a pack o' hungry dogs. Snapping. Snap. Snap. Tory, what am I seeing. They got guys on leashes, boygirls draggin em around on the dirty ce-ment floor. Somebody decides to capture it. Young men. Young women. They can't tell she's human. When is this happening. Tor. And someone will step back and take a snap. A shot. Aim. Shoot. Take.
That's what I'm seeing.

BEN: Believe me. // With all due respect … It's REALLY temporary.

JAY: Our wanting to be here. Is no.

BEN: Well, we just want to snap a coupla pics. And hang out. Get a feel for things. We'll worry about reporting back later.

Ben and Andrew glare at each other. Andrew instinctively puts a protective hand over one of Tory's breasts.

TORY: Worshipper Led By a Goddess Toward an Enthroned God.
Goddess and God in Attendance with Nude Female Between.
Worshipper Carrying Kid Before Sun God with Goddess and Goat Above;
Demonic Mask, Bull, Human Head, Star and Crescent.

Tory, as she's saying the inscriptions, places her hand protectively over Andrew's breast. As a result, his own protective hand slowly falls away from her breast. He looks to Tory. Tory looks at Ben. Her other hand gropingly grips the back of Andrew's neck, and massages it. She glares, glares, glares into the distance that begins just beyond Ben's left ear and extends far, far beyond. Over the fields and hills and past the towns and the cities and the ports and across the ocean beyond, into a great expanse that is invisible and unknowable, but which she yet sees and knows.

Sunday Best

Jay is taking pictures of their dirty feet.

JAY: Yes, the shadows will perhaps accentuate the dirt on the feet, or perhaps the light from the door hole will do it better. Yes, hold the child like that. Thank you and …
Snap!

LINDA: Well, Sunday will be here in a few days and actually we get scrubbed up and we put on our newer clothes. How about some nice pictures of <u>that</u>?

EVERYBODY: POOF!

TORY: Yeah, and we can all line up and stand in a nice neat line together, and we'll be ready for the pics, how about it, and then you can make them? Because otherwise then all you're doing is snapping us when we're not ready, when the day's a mess and everybody's tired and dirty.

JAY: We have come to snap you when the moment calls and we see something of the significance that desires to be snapped and captured and told as an image. That's when.

LINDA: We can't have any – not *any*? – where we are standing up nice and straight and tall with scrubbed hands and brushed teeth and combed hair // and starched collars and fetching frocks on our day of rest? When we are fresh from rest and worship?

STEVE: Pressed pants!

BEN: Oh, all right.

JAY: I will take one on Sunday.

BEN: *(Caressingly.)* If it'll // shut you up.

JAY: If this will make you happy

LINDA: Yeah, yes … that … helps

EVERYBODY: POOF!

Dream of the Machines

STEVE: *(Telling the guys and telling the audience and anyone else who will listen.)* Ok. About those machines. If you want to be an American machinist, and I do – why, I had a cousin who worked for the Sperry Gyroscope Company, ever heard of em? He worked as an Inspector in the Inspection department of their Marine Division. He'd tell us all sorts of different elements of doing machine work. So from him I know a thing or two by and by. He was a cousin, and I'd like to get an opportunity somewhere, maybe not so much around here, but somewhere around, where I could fix up a little shop of my own. Nothing big. Nothing like Sperry Gyroscope, but just a little shop where I could get involved in some real machine work. It's good work. Good, solid work. And you're using your mind, and you're still working with your hands, and. And you're not breaking your back. In the meantime you don't need to break your back anymore.

EVERYBODY on 3: POOF!

STEVE: Alright. *(Clap! Rub!)* JUST BECAUSE I get the feeling you want to test me out. I'll tell you all there is that I know about machines and machine work. From my cousin, who we all knew and called as P.M. and his full name was Paul Milford Robinson. And I'm. Steve Robinson.

SONG: TORCH DESIGNS (SONG ABOUT MACHINES)

Torch designs
I'm really into torch designs
The thing is just that
you can do gas welding
you can do oxygen cutting
Right now it's the thing I'm most about
Right now it's the thing I'm thinking most about
Hello! Hello.

But you need to have the right tools
Purchase them with money
Barter them with something
Borrow them be careful
Torches, blow pipes, mixers tips
Torches, blow pipes, mixers tips
Hello! Hello.

Torch seam weld
Acetylene
Heating valve
Connection nut
Torch rear end
and nipple hose nut
connection nut
See what I mean it's sexy!

You got to admit it's sexy!
Hello! Hello.

Butt weld flash weld projection weld spot weld
molten push up pressure
after welding resistance welds
forces molten metal
See what I mean it's sexy!
You got to admit it's sexy!
Hello! Hello.

Control, design
high production speeds
Nugget size, the trigger tip
Upset the butt welding
Grip the butted pieces
See what I mean it's sexy!
You got to admit it's sexy!

Some Solitary Region

Jay is taking pictures of Tory. He's making her stand in super bright blinding light.

SARAH: Squinting Woman Before Rutted House Boards Biting Lower Lip in Blinding Sunlight.

EVERYBODY: Click. Snap. POOF!

JAY: There's something about you that I love.
So you see there's ever more than meets the eyes.

TORY: *(Grumbling, mumbling.)* Crowned Hero Grasping Mule.
Nude Bearded Hero Holding Human-Headed Mules.
Nude Bearded Hero Wrestling with Water Buffalo Bull.

Shuffle shuffle.

BEN: Ahem. //
We are interested in your life, in what your life is.
We wonder if you ever had any hopes. Did you ever have any "*hope*"? That you can remember?

TORY: Bull Man Overpowering Lion.
Nude Bearded Hero Subduing Bull.

TORY: *(Cont'd.)* I don't know what you mean.
Only what we see and what we can't yet see. // There's no difference.

STEVE: *(Suddenly seeing.)* Drill bits! Tiny drill bits and you use them to pierce into stones and chisel out a mark! That mean something – or a thought that finds you. And you mark it out with these pointed drill bits!

EVERYBODY: POOF!

Planting Day Prophecy

BEN: How is it do you feel that you are helping the earth?

LINDA: Oh. Here. Let me show you.

Takes some seeds.

SARAH: Here's the next seeds. You'd think we just put em in the ground, like tiny corpses. Or soak them in water overnight. Nope. That's not the way we do it. We kind of have to hide the way we do it. Ok, nobody's looking. The coast is clear ...

BEN: Okay. What are you doing?

Linda puts some of the seeds in her mouth.

Puts some of the seeds in her kid's mouth.

Puts some of the seeds in her husband's mouth.

LINDA: This is what.

Holds them there.

BEN: Um. Do you think I can I have some in my mouth too?

Puts some in his mouth too.

Hold the seeds in the mouths for a while so as to let them absorb the information about their bodies, their blood, their fluids, their chemicals, any sicknesses, that kind of thing.

Take the seeds out of the mouth.

SARAH: Ok.

Hold the seeds out in the hands, in view of the heavens above. Take off the shoes or any foot wrappings. Let the information from the sweat on the feet transfer itself into the soil. At the same time hold the hands out that contain the seeds in them so that they can communicate with the planets and other celestial bodies. And they have a chance to transfer the information that they have learned to the planets and stars so that they can do their part to help everything along and grow into health for those human bodies.

SARAH: This is our prayer. Ok. Got it? Let's plant them.

Plant them in the ground.

Tory comes back out.

TORY: What's up you guys.

They startle as if caught in an amorous embrace.

BEN: This is intimacy with the earth.

SARAH: Yes. It's hard to see, but it's a great deal.

BEN: Ahem. I'll go and get the watering can!

SARAH: No. *(Hand on arm to prevent.)* We don't actually water them for three nights. They need to hang on to our information for a while that they've just gathered. Then we'll give em a good soakin.

TORY: Quick let's do some more.

Sun God Rising with Attendants Opening the Gates of Heaven.

Leading Gods Bringing Birdman for Judgment.

The Shepherd Who Ascends to Heaven and Consolidates All the Foreign Countries's

Flight to Heaven on the Back of an Eagle.

Three Demons Whose Legs Are Foreparts of Merged Lions Whose Tails End in Serpent Heads. Check.

Ok. These are pretty big ones. Let's take a break. Everybody just take a minute to stretch and relax, and rest for a second.

Resting. Without privacy but and on the other hand, with uncommon physical modesty.

Linda comes back out.

LINDA: Get back to work!

SARAH: Everything's planted. Nothing to do til chopping and sweeping now.

LINDA: Oh yes there is.

TORY: Ok. Ready everybody? Let's get back to it.

Satisfied that they mean something of the same thing by "work" and certain they are really going to resume right away, and anyway thinking about her own stuff, Linda goes back in.

They do resume.

TORY: Let's dim all the lights. Way down.

The lights dim way down. They enter an ecstasy of inscriptions. Steve and Sarah assisting in abstract but necessary gestural illustrations. Ben joins awkwardly, inadequately.

TORY: Bull Man Fighting Lion; Nude Bearded Hero Kneeling on a Lion and Holding a Lion Griffin Behind His Head; check.

Corkscrew-eared Bunny Demon (yes, that's definitely a bunny this time, bro!)

Worshipper Holding Hare Before Enthroned Male Figure, Vultures Above.

STEVE: You betcha. Check.

TORY: Weather God with Helmet Standing on Mountains, Brandishing Heavy Club and Holding Snake, Frog Pond Blossom, and Rein of Kneeling Bull Surmounted by Nude Goddess Opening Veil.

STEVE: Check. Where are those kids? Let's wipe em up so we can get em out here an see!

TORY: Nude Bearded Hero with Flowing Streams Flanked by Winged Lion Demons.

God with Lightning Fork and Foot on Bull.

SARAH: Click.

TORY: Goats Before a Shrine; Pigtailed Figures with Vessels; Cows Lying on Mountains.
Nude Winged Goddess Holding Two Antelopes.
Two Fish Men with Pollen Baskets Flanking Sacred Tree; God in Winged Sun Disk Above.

STEVE: Snap. SNAP!

TORY: Large Mass of Half Cloud Half Sandy Beach, Jeweled Wisps of Fish, Tranquil Sleep-Belly-Dancing Mother Superior, Jewel-Encrusted Fishes, Golden Boats and Bearded Tadpoles Washing Up On Shore, Deep, Clear Waters, Pink Spectral Evidence of Paleocontact. Check. Mother Waters. Milky Jewel-Feeding Waters.
Choice of Immortality. Opt-out. Check.

STEVE: Check. Check. Check. Check. Check.

BEN: She's nuts!

JAY: The most abandoned of all of these people. She is lost in some solitary region of her own.

SARAH: These are a way of praying Tory can do. We just follow along.

Prophecy.

STEVE: Oilcloth tablecloth.

Paper suitcase.

Truck without a floor.

Lemonade for eight made with two lemons, no ice, tepid spring water, and very sweet.

SARAH: I got one, y'all: Mile Upon Mile Upon Mile Upon Mile, Mid-July While Cotton is Making. Nineteen Shack-Buildings-of-Crooked-Wooden-Pieces-Resting-on-Stacked-Stones-Which-Could-Be-Pushed-Flat-By-One-Man-Who-Tried-Hard Dark-Shaded-Porches in Twenty: Whole Family, Blank Eyes Like Fish, Seated in Stiff Rows Speechless, Slack as Meats on Butcher Hooks, More Dead Than Death in the Dead Weeks Before Picking: Adolescent Daughters in Cleanest Happiest Prints. What about that? How's that?

Linda comes back out.

LINDA: In the morning, before picking time comes, after Andrew force feeds himself eggs and lard and hardtack biscuits and gets his boots on and heads out toward the field where he's working that day, before we follow him to break our own backs under the finality of the noon sun, we will take the little ones out to see what of these sprouts have come up.

SARAH: I'll go and find them. By the way, I know what is happening. And it's very sad. And it's happening to me too.

Exeunt, looking up at the sky.

Ben and Jay are left alone.

BEN: Who are we reporting this for? Is this American? Who are our superiors? Which direction?
How do I describe them – these deceived and captured? How can I how can I do them justice?

JAY: It's not justice. Not any more the scales that weigh their bales at the cotton engine are the scales of justice. There is no place for justice here – only justification. Either you give up the very clothing on your back or you justify. If we take. If we make beautiful. We justify. *(He lights up a smoke.)* Don't you sleep? Don't you change your suit?

BEN: What if I am falling in love with them? What does that justify?

JAY: Pssssss. In order to love, we are unjust.

BEN: If I have been unjust, it is only because I loved.

Dramatic exit.

JAY: Psssssss. He enters the church for to be worshipped by it.

He grinds out his cigarette in self-contempt.

Fallen Star

Jean Ann has returned, wearing furs and gloves and loose unraveled sequins and hatboxes and strings of pearls which are all dusty and haggard by Broadway standards but here stand out like the most glamorous fashions of the day imaginable. She is telling Sarah all about what it's like out in the world – the entertainment world.

JEAN ANN: And they served little plates of tiny pickles and the tiniest forks you had ever seen to eat them with.

SARAH: Are those REAL character shoes?! Are those JAZZ!!???

EVERYBODY: POOF!

JEAN ANN: And then one time I got invited to the home of a real BARON! // for lunch! A home cooked meal in the middle of a tour of twelve plus cities! Imagine it! We had some of the finest lambchops // and there were two real manservants who served it. And potatoes cooked in just a marvelous way and asparagus and greens, and at the end you had to choose between coffee and tea and I couldn't! The cups for coffee and the cups for tea were so beautiful and in different ways! I wanted all of it! To stay there for days and days and enjoy everything there was to have in that house!

SARAH: Gasp! You don't say!

SARAH: Lambchops!

A jig. Maybe a sad, mournful one. During the jig, she sees that Sarah's legs are f'd up.

JEAN ANN: Is that from the cart 'accident'?

SARAH: Yeah. It got worse.

JEAN ANN: Oh, that didn't happen to me! One thing that DID happen that shall haunt me until the day one of us dies – either me or the Baron. I belched! I belched at the table! Oh oh oh oh oh oh oh – I was minding my table manners, I swear I was! And I was doing very well on the conversation, though I wasn't very relaxed, and the food really was very very very good and then it just came out! Just like a little word of something – except that it was an ugly little belch. I knew I had spoiled everything. Everything in my life.

When I find out that he's on his deathbed I'm going to rush there and throw myself down on my knees at his bedside and beg for his forgiveness.

Oh! And the most important thing that I forgot to tell you is that when they served the tea and the coffee the spoons were very old – and had little stained glass windows in them – each one! In the SPOON part!! I'll never ever get over that, not as long as I live.

She shakes her head in wonder and amazement just thinking about it.

Up until then I didn't know that there were people in the world who sat through things with their lives and the gratification of their basic wants tucked neatly around them like small pillows on a sofa.

His interest in me was one of the great kindnesses paid to me of my whole life – to me it was …

Another sad jig.

SONG: FOLLIES (SONG ABOUT A LIFE IN SHOWBIZ THE SHE PULLS SARAH IN ON)

Chicago, Saint Louis
Little Rock
Kansas City
Buffalo
And I, well I, forget some too.
California
Chattanooga
Jackson
San Antone
And I, well I, am trying to forget some too.

These are just some
of the places we know
Where you can join
the Follies

Somebody's Follies
Somebody or other
travel in a motor coach.
And forget everything else
in your hotel room.

One of these days I'm gonna be Franch
I'm telling you
Franch kisses, Franch fries, Franch bread!
Coffee and smokes, layin' in bed
I'm telling you
put somma that old time tunes!
and I'll go real quiet and my name could be
I'm telling you
my name could be Clara!
and I could be fierce, and talk with my mouth
I'm telling you
mouth full of pages of books!
and keep a glass pot of apricot
of apricot jam on my bed tray!

Forget the creek
forget the talks
forget the walks
forget the tall companion
and the song about the whispering grass.

Busted-up Hot Tubs and Prayers to the Deaf Heavens

Jay takes a break. He speaks abstractedly to whichever of the women is around. Linda? Tory? Sarah? He gazes distractedly at the busted-up hot tub languishing in the dry tangled grass.

JAY: The first Atelier at which I studied was as a prison to my sensibilities. *(Truthfully.)* Yes, I too am a dreamer.

In this world of nature there are positive force and evil forces. Where evolution is unrestrained and helped by a positive force, there is beauty. If the victory goes to the evil force, or to the obstacle of free evolution, then ugliness prevails. This is what we have here, on the surface, in the immediate impression, in this squalor. Abject squalor on the surface. But if we cut into it as a surgeon puts the knife to the skin, we find something else when we have opened its flesh. And by cutting it open I mean … that we see it. Here we see the victory of all obstacles. Here we have what has been one of man's greatest creations, the Jacuzzi hot tub, –

STEVE: *(Interrupting.)* Developed by the incredible inventors of machine propellers and water pumps, the seven Jacuzzi brothers. That's Full Foam Insulation, hoss. A miracle of modern technology and a symbol of status and superiority of mankind.

JAY: And look at it, chopped up into many piece with a mechanical saw or some such apparatus // and left out at the side of the road for the rubbish collectors to clean up. Tangled in the grass that is so dry.

STEVE: A 'Saws-All'!!

STEVE: Except that you're wrong about one thing – nothing is ever wasted or discarded as rubbish on a farm. Look at the coils of wires and rusted buckets piled up in the one corner of the porch. These things may come to some use later on.

JAY: I will dig and dive all the way into this realitée, into its full darkness, and I won't cry and wail and grovel at their feet as Ben. I can look without loving and love without dying. I can lift and push hard against this realitée. I can become the positive force, that will overcome the pitiless squalor and raise this wretched grubbiness and foul dilapidation to a state of passionate suffering. To beauty raise. You will see.

JEAN ANN: In my showbiz dream career I have been made so happy on an appearance on Queen for a Day and I won this wonderful Jacuzzi spa hot tub. Other than that, I didn't have a penny to my name. They said, 'Where do you want it, JAGSTAR?' So I had it sent back here, in hopes that it would raise the status here, and show that we've had our good times too.

SARAH: We ended up chopping it up because its pipes got jammed with a bunch of dirt and hair and dead grass. We didn't know how to fix it. And we didn't know about any Jacuzzi repair experts in the area, so.

JAY: *(To Steve.)* You can't do something to repair it? With all your interest in machines?

STEVE: There might be something in that corner of the porch I can use … someday …

Andrew comes across the field.

SARAH: Um …

TORY: Andrew's back.

LINDA: Help git that supper on the table, will you Jean Ann.

Nobody does anything. The heat is paralyzing.

Andrew enters. He looks at the scene. He undoes one button of his overalls.

ANDREW: What's she doing here.

EVERYBODY: POOF!

LINDA: She came to stay here with family. Things just got to be too much for her, I guess.

ANDREW: She gonna work?

TORY: Course she's gonna work.

Jean Ann stares. Nods. Stares at Andrew. Stares at Linda. Stares at Tory. Stares at Sarah.

ANDREW: Well, welcome back then.

He puts down his stuff.

JEAN ANN: It stinks in here. It smells sour. I'm glad it's my own family or I wouldn't be able to stand it. There's a certain smell your own family has that even when it's bad it comforts you. That's not true of the places I've stayed out there on the road, after you've been on the hot road – in the hot dust – and the blinding heat, all the damn night and day shoved in right next to somebody else on the bumps, last night's wine dried on their lips, and you feel a little queasy … you can't relax cause it's got that sour milk smell and a bad old carpet wall to wall with everything from thousands of people's bodies and skins and scabs and streets mashed down into it. It's not any cooler inside than outside, the carpet is sticky and you hear your slippers peeling off of it every time you lift your foot to take a step; and you don't want to touch a single thing in there. And somehow you've got to find a way to <u>sleep</u> in there. The sweat from a thousand different heads on a thousand sweaty miserable sweltering nights baked into the pillows, drying there in the noon, making them stale? Stiff? and nasty. Same thing here. But there: worse. Everything on the cheap. Crumbling at the edges. Brown and gummy in the cracks. Other people's hairs in the towels and on the lump of soap. And it's not your family. So it's that much worse.

Andrew goes over to Jean Ann.

ANDREW: Well, you stay as long as you need to, sister kitten. You'll sleep right in there with me and Tory. Don't you worry.

He kisses her on the cheek. Looks at her. Tory sees, Linda sees. Linda looks at Tory. Andrew kisses Jean Ann on the mouth. Tory goes outside taking a bucket and a baby with her. Andrew sits down at the table. Everybody else sits down too. Tory comes back in, the bucket full of water. Sits down with the baby on her lap.

SARAH: Here in these parts we end up not so religious with regard to much, except in stormfear and fear of death. There used to be occasional Sunday meetings at our closest neighbor's house out near where there's talk of paving the road, and we all looked forward and everyone came, but scornful outsiders started to come and the meetings got too rough. But before every dinner and supper we do pray to the deaf heavens before we eat of what is not very much.

They say grace to the deaf heavens

"Hello?"

"HELLO??"

"Anybody there?"

"Uh … thanks?"

"Thanks for this and uh …"

"Help?"

"Yeah HELP!?"

"HELP!"

"HELP US!"

"Please Help Us!!"

"Amen."

EVERYBODY: POOF!

And eat.

Dinner is over quickly. There's not much food. Andrew and the men go out onto the porch. The women clean up.

EVERYBODY: POOF!

Pickling Day

Jean Ann is doing some kitchen work with the women that also holds the meaning that she is re-joining them in their ways and concerns. In this case it's pickling some lumpy brown pickles. The story we hear is mostly the last thing we'll hear her say of her showbiz days. She keeps trying to make it so that Ben will hear what she's saying and make her famous somehow. But he is never listening. He's always working on something else, probably organizing notes that he frantically took while Tory was talking, or Linda. Here is where she gives up. Jay is polishing up and maintaining his photography equipment as Steve looks on with great interest. Also Jean Ann is taking her clothes off, her roadshow traveling city-to-city clothes, using each piece for a different kitchen task, and then putting each away in her paper suitcase, revealing a very simple ad hoc shift underneath.

JEAN ANN: … and we saw them up ahead of us on the beach, and when we caught up to them, the man, who had silver hair turned around, and it was George Hamilton!

SARAH: No! Was he tan?!

JEAN ANN: Of course he was! It was George Hamilton! And the whitest teeth I'd ever seen before or since. He had a sort of sardonic, condescending sort of smile.

There is difficulty shoving a particularly unwieldy pickle down the neck of a narrow-mouthed jar, requiring assistance.

LINDA: Just shove it in there Jean Ann.

SARAH: It doesn't want to go, Mama!

JEAN ANN: *(Setting the big pickle aside.)* I might as well tell you about the Baron-*ess* I visited too. She had servants. I was there as a servant also. You do what you gotta do. And she had a much younger husband, and she was a beautiful older woman and their house was very very open and had some very very expensive looking antiques in it, and china plates, and – I was not there as a guest, but the vibe everyone was giving was that I was a guest. It was a fine line for me to walk. I sat at the table with them. I was included as a guest even though everyone knew I was a student. I mean servant. And there were cut-open seashells mixed in with the concrete of the patio where the table was,

STEVE: *(Jolted by this image away from Jay and his equipment and stumbling halfway across the room.)* What do you mean? How did they do that? Machines! Had to be! What machines!?

JEAN ANN: *(Cont'd.)* and it was unbelievably pleasant to sit there because of the breezes and the exact right temperature of the air. And the butlers came around serving the food which was very very good and tasty, and if the Baroness didn't want any of a particular dish she merely turned her head away from the dish as it was offered to her. Almost in disgust. Which was fascinating to me.

EVERYBODY: POOF!

ANDREW: Say, uh, Jean Ann?

JEAN ANN: Hi, Andrew. Thanks for letting me stay.

ANDREW: Well, you're family, aren't ye?

JEAN ANN: Yeah, but. I know you don't have to. So.

ANDREW: What about yr husband? What did he have to say?

JEAN ANN: Hasn't said. Haven't heard. He's the one who sent me off in the first place and I was glad enough to go.

ANDREW: *(Stroking her hair and running his fingers through it.)* He treats you mean, he gets jealous, he got jealous, // and then he couldn't stand it anymore.

TORY: Andrew, I see you. Knock it off.

He knocks it off.

JEAN ANN: He couldn't. He sent me off. It's all right by me. I like and prefer the towns. I like and prefer the other young people who are so soft. *(Now speaking very loud for Ben's benefit.)* I like the way the heel of my shoe feels when it's wrapped around the brass foot rail at the big long bar of a city chophouse. *(Music begins.)* Hook me in, Charlie, and set me up a drink. Scoot the bill over on down to my pal Johnny here – is it Johnny? Or is it Jimmy? That's fiiiine.

SONG: FOLLIES (REPRISE)

(That she tries to get Ben's attention with.)

Chicago, St. Louis, Little Rock
Where people are blowin their horns
Motor horns and trombones for good reason

Cincinnati, Mil-a-waukee
Where you can join somebody's Follies
Cliff Hamdie's, Silas Green, or Charleston Chewy's
And forget everything else in your hotel room.

BEN: *(Ignoring her, typing.)* But this I observe, I observe them using the split flour sacks like this
For blankets, for towels, for stockings.
There's something mysterious in how white they can be.
I thank God for them in this hot sun heat with their light blue letters.

Jean Ann gives up and sings a song of resignation to less than ideal circumstances.

SONG: LITTLE PICKLES

Now I am here and I can work again
In the fields the kitchen brother husband sister friend
Wash the supper dishes so greasy from the pork
(Men: While we smoke out on the porch)

Oh, those little pickles!
Fancy stained glass window spoons
Now just brown amorphous pickles
Soggy shadows in the gloom
Til after our ever after
I'll never get a little pickle again.

Scarcity of butter and shortage of eggs
Big fat ugly pickles like if jellyfish had legs
Talk a little talk in the fading light – coming of the night

I'll dream little pickles!
Fancy stained glass window spoons
These old vague misshapen pickles
I could throw them across the room
Til after, our ever after
I'll never get a little pickle again.

BEN: *(To Jean Ann.)* I'm now grown fond of you. And I'm very sorry for you.

If you come out onto the porch. The front of your dress and their dresses soaked with dishwater. The crickets, the night-birds, the locusts.

For a few minutes, everything easing up for a few minutes of leisure.

She looks at him. Andrew looks between them, Tory looks at Andrew, Andrew sees Tory looking at him. He looks down at the table. Silence and then silence narrated by Andrew, gritting his teeth and still looking down at the table but then getting up and narrating the silence from the outskirts.

SONG: PERSON TO PERSON

(Andrew sings, a one-man chorus of jealousy.)

Ah uh uh
Ah uh uh

A holiness happens that is his
So she pulls at him for closer

Person to person
Human to human
To love, to love
Thinking of, thinking of

he holds her fixed distance away
fixed then not too far away. They are safe.

Bedroom. Bedroom.
Room to bed.
Foot to Head to Foot, to Head.
In bed, Foot to Head.

He walks next to her. They climb on the rocks. She knows and begins to know ringing. Ringing reaches upward. // He is one person. // She is one person.

TORY: Andrew.

TORY: Cut.

TORY: The shit.

ANDREW:

> *I Love, My Love.*
> *Ah uh uh.*
> *Ah uh uh.*
> *(Whistling.)*

Tory returns to a previous subject, but it's still this subject. But the narrated silence is over for now. Andrew returns to the shadows.

TORY: You know, it's true. That there's only so much strength in a day.

Ben hears Tory. He leaves off being fond of Jean Ann, creeps up and begins writing along with her talking, with gestures and flourishes to denote that he is copying it all down beautifully and with great human feeling.

TORY: When we were young, we had more strength to fight it, to live, get it all done, like heroes, and laugh at our position in life. Cause what did it matter if we were so gloriously alive? Work in the fields all day and at the end of the day come back here and clean up the whole place, take care of all the kids, and men like you *(Ben)* driving up in cars to ask about me at the end of those days. And I always said, 'No, thank you.' I didn't leave my family. Now that I stayed, my daughters are all my sisters and my sons are all my brothers. I have brothers who are nephews and sisters who are nieces.

LINDA: We stayed together.

TORY: I stayed home instead of leaving with one of those men.

LINDA: This is what happened after that.

TORY: We are graced and cursed by our *(she clears her throat)* for the land.

Women fists shaken against the sky. "We'll never go hungry again." ("Except that we're totally starving right now.") Ben continues writing – typing – with elaborate ornaments of gesture, then furiously, mouthing the words also with great passion.

TORY: *(Cont'd.)* Depending on how you look at it.

LINDA: *(In secret confidence.)* Though not all the babies can stay to become people, to work with us ...

TORY: When the births happen, our hearts reach out in so many different ways.

ALL THE WOMEN: Reach beyond all boundaries.

TORY: This is procreation and we are astonished by the truth that is revealed to us by it.

THE FAMILY: There are no strangers here.

LINDA: Those of us who birth have been seen born by everyone in the room. We are the ones who are still here.

TORY: The empty space between us emphasizes our gestures, and holds so much more than carnality. We are framed by animals that we know, and by animals we have never seen before.

EVERYONE: We fall down on our knees and weep with confusion and gratitude.

Fallen down on knees and weeping with confusion and gratitude.

Jean Ann stands up and opens a letter from her husband.

JEAN ANN: This letter ... I've received this letter, you see ... My husband, well he ... it seems that I ....

Her weeping is crying. She cries and tries to powder her face.

LINDA: Well, I guess she's being sent for.

JEAN ANN: I'm to meet a man with a truck who'll drive me as far as Fayetteville.

TORY: A man who's coming toward this way to pick up a dresser and a bed frame. A man we don't know.

Lemonade for eight is made. The making of it echoes the seed-ceremony somehow. Once it is over, Jean Ann faces Jay and Ben. Sarah behind them.

JEAN ANN: How come you never came to find me!

JAY & BEN: But I did – I chased you! Didn't you see me?

JAY: I ran and ran after that truck // that day.

BEN: The truck with no floor. // Your paper suitcase in the back, your slippers resting on the hot engine.

JAY: You just kept your hand on your hat to keep it from blowing off.

JAY & BEN: I had love for you.

BEN: I had love for you that I didn't give you // and I didn't want you to leave without it.

JAY: Also, I did grab you into my arms when we were standing outside talking and saying goodbye and exchanging // thanks and appreciations and gratitudes.

BEN: I did, after all, after not doing, I did do it.

JEAN ANN: Oh, I felt it, I guess.

I watched it float away like a cloud or a fog into the white noon as I lay crushed and smothered in my husband's unfeeling of me embrace unfeeling of me. I became me and not I.

The women cry in each others' arms, or are stoic. Steve stands with his arm around Linda, they look on. Jean Ann turns to go and meet the man they don't know, with the truck without a floor.

JEAN ANN: How lovely to have a flower named after one. Goodbye.

Night Day Night Day Night Day

TORY: Somebody, somebody big, and strong, carries me over to a sacred cedar tree and lays me down at the foot of it. The work I have done for the earth today, that will never be recognized in my lifetime, is recognized and appreciated here in these arms that lay me at the foot of this sacred holy magical cedar tree. Every night. Before I fall off the cliff into black sleep. I've got no blood left almost, and then here we go.

SONG: BLACK, BLACK SLEEP

THE FAMILY:

A black black sleep
carries me over to a cedar tree
that's holy, lays me down
Somebody, somebody
big and strong,
that's holy, lays me down

A black black sleep
My blood is gone,
all of my blood has gone
and then here, here we go.
Every night all my lifetime,
and then here, here we go.

A black, black, sleep.
A black, black, sleep.
A black, black, sleep.

Darkroom Revelation

Some time later, a small rented darkroom in the Big City, lit by a single red lightbulb.

Ben is in an adjoining room, typing and editing like crazy.

JAY: Here I am in this rented darkroom again. Ah, but it is good to get back to the Big City, enjoying the culture, the beautiful women, the brusque, irreverent parties again. Let us see … How did the photographs come out from our summer report with the tenant farmer families. Hmm … What?

Wait a minute – *These* photographs I never took! These over here I did – in this tub. Yes. These of the wagon and the dirt-smeared children – sure, sure – quite extraordinary in their composition I might add –

But THESE! No, they are on the same roll of film but is impossible that I took these!

There are only a few of them, but they are full of some strange *passiòn etrangé* and hidden meaning – oh! Ah! They speak to me alone!

SONG: L'IMAGE

L'Image
On voie, en vue, on joue dans les soirées

Les soirées!

L'Image!

Shaded Death Dream

Flagrant, Daemonic Beauty – so bright and vivid!

Light and Darkness, Water Sky – Smoke! Strange Balloons – *Ballons Étrangé* –

L'Image

Les bêtes, les larmes, des enfants mes fortées

Mes fortées!

L'Image!

Plus also plus the Formal Relationship –

Un Loup, un rougarou, le Pompidou, loup garou.

Un Loup, un rougarou, le Pompidou, loup garou.

L'Image!

sob, sob – between with Blurry and – and – and –

the All-Too-Specific. They are a message – for me!

I am overcome!

One moment please …

He is feverish, sweated and deeply shaken.

He takes a moment to compose himself. He searches for his handkerchief in the darkness and mops his forehead.

Harp music.

He is sobbing, gasping for air.

It's too much – it's too MUCH! Ah, GOD!
What does it MEAN I DON'T KNOW WHAT IT MEANS!!

He drops to his knees.
He weeps into his handkerchief until it is sopping wet. He whimpers.

I feel I can almost recognize in these an order of deep visual meaning which I receive only by divine universal providence.

L'eau ciel
L'eau ciel
L'eau ciel
L'eau ciel
L'eau ciel

SUSAN SONTAG: The photographs you have taken, on the other hand, seem to ensure that you will not have to be renting a darkroom for much longer.

JAY: What! Who are you! What woman! What is this!?

SUSAN SONTAG: Bobby. You don't remember me?

JAY: No. Should I?

SUSAN SONTAG: This is what we call a visitation, young photographer. Nevermind about me or who I am. Believe me, you're not ready to know. *(She lights up a smoke and has a look around.)* I miss New York. *(To the audience.)* I miss you guys. Though it's all gone to shit as a cultural center, hasn't it, a shadow of what it once was. I still miss you …

JAY: But what has this got to do with my renting this darkroom–

SUSAN SONTAG: With these, you are no longer a reporter, no longer a vessel for the truth. The impact of their contrasts, the punctum, the admittedly impeccable technical composition, you might almost say that they are beyond criticism. Well, until I come along, anyway. Much later. In the SEVENTIES. For now at least, who could question their beauty, their unflinchingness at the subjects they depict? These photographs you have taken will rocket you to tremendous artistic success and, with it, immortality.

JAY: What!

SUSAN SONTAG: Calm down. It's the same with your typewriter friend and his florid, poetic language. Now let's look at these other ones that have got you so freaked out – those which you don't remember taking: what do they show?

JAY: They depict something like the images described to me by the family there – the ones they imagined carved in precious stones, saw embroidered on worn pinafores, and shed themselves, sewed them into the dry dirt of the earth over which they labored.

SUSAN SONTAG: Something of the consciousness and communication shared by humans, plants, animals and the earth, between wholeness for all beings – and they are not so easy to understand … are they?

Jay shakes his head, fighting back tears again.

SUSAN SONTAG: Look. I'll say it plainly. These pictures you took of the family are too beautiful to make us want to do anything to remedy their suffering –

To publish them will be to trap them in the burning hot cotton fields at the height of the picking season, with no cooling evening and no regenerative moonlight to restore them to the life of their inner souls. To make public these others will be to risk your reputation as a sane person of society, subject yourself to ridicule and worse – but to gain entrance to the secret reservoirs of ancient knowledge and redemption for humanity.

It seems to me, you've got a choice to make …

JAY: *(Jumping to his feet.)* Between moralitée and immortalitée–

SUSAN SONTAG: Between sleep-inducing beauty and the strangeness of truth …

JAY: Between the terrifying cycles of life and earth – versus the assurance that I and my photographs will disseminate such clear and beautiful images of pain and suffering through the generations, and will become as ubiquitous to the cultural eye as Christ himself on the crux, I choose –

Ben enters the darkroom and flips on the light switch, which exposes the images, ruining them.

JAY: Ah, shit! They are ruined!
Nevermind.
I make my choice.

He wheels around to face Ben.

JAY: Ben, good Christ, what is it that you have wrought at the typewriting machine? Do you in your artistic brilliance also stand at a crossroads?

BEN: Yeah. I'm editing it now. What I wrote was amazing.

They stand staring feverishly at one other, and begin to softly pant.

SUSAN SONTAG: And so, the tenant farming family we have come to know is dragged along in the wake of this choice, forced to abandon the consciousness sown and sewn into their patterns of fertility, birth, death, and earth with which they had so intimately identified.
It's too bad – much could have been saved.
Instead they are doomed to the eternal profanity of preserved death and endless life in a series of pretty pictures which slowly drain of impact on account of their overuse in an emerging mass culture as starved of meaning as these families were of food, education and opportunity –

She smokes.

SONG: YELLOW SHOES

You came here wearing yellow shoes
we didn't know we could refuse
Your claim to want to help. And now

it's we who lose.

BEN: Your suffering was really real
What were the terms of our appeal?
I only told what I could name,

'n' what I still feel.

LINDA: So say goodbye to blamelessness
Buh-bye to moral decency
ANDREW: For all your precious photographic evidence,
In the end you chose not to see!

JAY: Regarding the multitudes in disregard
One can't appeal to what's acquired

LINDA: Our pain could speak but we were weak
LINDA & ANDREW: We were

just too tired.

LINDA: You left our hearts just big empty holes
We knew no rest until we died
JAY: What we learned lay in what we stole
BEN: Concealed cause caused our lies

LINDA: (In the outro.) Trust
Left in the Dust
To the Grave
A few things Saved

The family turns and confronts Ben and Jay.

LINDA: Congratulations on your great success.

SARAH: How come you guys never came back?

TORY: We never even knew about the book.

JAY: We want you to know how much passionate respect we have for you humans and this, your predicament. All the others are aware, because we had it printed into these book.

BEN: And you know, FUCK EVERYONE who says it's a work of art!

JAY: Or journalísme! // FUCK them! FUCK time!

BEN: YEAH!

SARAH: It would have been nice if you just dropped by for a visit.

LINDA: I guess you never used those Sunday pictures we took ... Still ... You could have at least brought us a copy of the book, for gourd's sake.

BEN: But it didn't belong to any of us // anymore?

JAY: Not personally?

BEN: Nothing personal? Not to you or me // or …

JAY: the universe // as it hangs between us,

BEN: but to all the people outside our situation, // our poignant, poignant situation, and let them decide what to do about it.

JAY: Our poignant, poignant situation … We really posed that question to them as well: what are you going to do about this?

BEN: "What are you going to do with this? About it?"

SARAH: Did anyone ever do anything about it?

BEN: I don't they – did they?

ANDREW: No … people talked about it. People in town. Were whispering. Behind our backs. Somebody said laughing.

LINDA: But we never came to any better. I guess our grandchildren did … ?

JAY: There – see? Well, and thanks God for that!

BEN: Yeah!

TORY: Yeah, bro!

Pat, pat. Pat. Hard.

Paleocontact

TORY: You get one chance. Will you recognize it?

EVERYONE: You have seen our faces.

LINDA: This creek never ran behind the house where we lived.

STEVE: But it does now, in this new life.

TORY: Before we were tenant farmers, before we were clay eaters with hookworm in the hills, and before that. And before that. And before that. And before that. Mound builders.

EVERYONE: And our children after us.

ANDREW, TORY & JAY: Quiet fishing. Contemplation of the currents.

SARAH: The creek gathers here into a pool.

JEAN ANN: The water is cold and I can swim.

TORY: Deep, clear waters. Are these the mother waters?

SARAH: I can stand straight. I hear a slow song of whispering grass.

TORY: YEAH. Remember I was saying? Coming along to here on a boat? Through the reeds but not Moses? You come to a place ... You recognize it. But you're crying because you've never been here before, and it scares you. Look, there's that guy Ben. Crying in the water.

BEN: My third wife always said this project was like the ghost of a dead child to me. I ended up a drunk. I smashed a chair over a woman one time. Not her – another woman. But I can't believe I did that.

Andrew enters with his fishing pole. He sees Ben but doesn't say anything. City folk. He casts his line in.

TORY: This is only a reflection.

JEAN ANN: I found a job in a nursing home. I retired from there.

TORY: Look, there's Jay – remember him? There he is, even now, trying to photograph the currents.

Andrew shakes his head.

JAY: I look for what is invisible in the currents, and trying to understand by capturing it. My life was an endeavor to place the visible at the service of the invisible.

SARAH: How green and lush everything is. We could have lived a life, instead of just survived, just barely.

JEAN ANN: I am bathing in the pool – the water is very cold. Ha ha ha h-ha.

SARAH: Because this is where the spring comes in and feeds it – double spring, from both sides.

Jean Ann gets into the hot tub, which is now whole and sparkling with bright tiles. The sound is of rapid atrial fibrillation detected in echocardiogram and amplified.

JEAN ANN: Oh, now THIS is WONDERFUL!

Enter Linda, into the hot tub.

LINDA: The whole experience of life might have fallen apart, but damn I love this hot tub.

SARAH: It's whole again! Look at those sparkling bright tiles!

LINDA: Oh, Steve! Nice work.

STEVE: *(He waves.)* I love you, honey.

TORY: What we find in the unfolded, opening up ways.

A dog runs across.

TORY: Jean Ann has looked up and seen something preternatural that is in the water.

JEAN ANN: Remember that embroidered skirt scene?

SARAH: Tender scene? Family standing by the stream?

TORY: Look at Andrew he sees. And so does Sarah. Drift. Yeah and you also saw the huge carp appear in the darker water toward the bottom. You didn't think there were fish that big in this little pool.

ANDREW: No …

TORY: It scares you a little.

ANDREW: Yeah …

TORY: Because it's like a human …

SARAH: Only much older …

TORY: This is where and how a visitation comes. It gets manifested just like this. It's profound, but it's easy to miss.

ANDREW: Fish-Carp-Man Visitation

TORY: Yep. Yep, honey.

SARAH: Fish-Carp-Man-Eagle Gripping Nothing, Stabbing Nothing. Backed By Orbs, Pods, And Vessels.

JEAN ANN: It came to the surface, it is like a man, but now flying above us? *(To the Carp-Man-Eagle.)* What is now? I can't place you – you're not from around here, are you? From water? From air? Who are you?

JEAN ANN: We get near this being and our minds work at the speed they were meant to.

TORY: Which is what? Very, very fast?

JEAN ANN: Yes.

STEVE: I knew it!

JEAN ANN: I profess to understand what this being is saying to us.

TORY: You look so human.

JEAN ANN: You rise to the surface to meet me, and so I go along with you halfway into the sky.

LINDA: I see you off. Embrace us – the sun rests for a moment in a blue disk.

JEAN ANN: I am flying too, in the pink sky water, seeing the golden boats on the surface above, the ceiling of the atmosphere, on the surface of the sea below and the bottom below that in the waving seaweeds. The choice to live forever or just for now is not given to me.

Andrew enters with the guitar. He sings with Linda.

SONG: A SONG OF TRYING TO REMEMBER (REPRISE)

I learned to trust
When I did not have pillow
I lay in the dust
My grave they dug too shallow
How can we say what future they ~~won't~~ remember?

When grandsons hum this song, call it 'See You In September'?

The enormous Bird Carp Man flies through. Sarah stumbles on the rocks. Jean Ann stumbles on the rocks. She and Tory gaze at each other.

ADAPA: Hi, it's me again. I go by Adapa in some other parts of the world. Though I was here too, and you have remembered me.

JEAN ANN: But I'm not even born yet!

SARAH: And saw then I, swimming in the deep part in this way that made me know the deepest dark rushing red rocky water, carp-fish, man, tall, with flat palms I think, gentle reservation accommodating, me. Eagle I can't see you but you're clear as day.

(To Adapa.) You heard me, my prayer. Adapa.

ADAPA: I went up to mountains – I was looking for the plant of birth. Plant of life. I didn't find. Some bunch of white dudes tore down one of my temple mounds. The land is now flat, with tire treads clearly visible in the dirt. To put up a Sam's Club they're saying.

SARAH: Oh.

ADAPA: I tell you what. Though? If you want I can take you to where you might find.

SARAH: Oh. Where?

ADAPA: Up …

Up.

SARAH: I can't. I cannot leave here.

ADAPA: Okay. Well, maybe some other time, then. So long.

SARAH: Everything I know is stored in the plants that grow on the earth, that we planted, that we cared for, that we picked. If you carry those seeds to where the plant of life is growing … it gives our generations.

TORY: Carp-fish rising, man, //eagle, I know you in my dream, you make perfect understanding of me, you disclose the design of the land. Why do you disclose to us wretched humankind the ways of heaven and earth?

SARAH: Adapa!

LINDA: And what can we do for you?

JEAN ANN: And he dives back down and disappears.

SARAH: And he flies away into the sky. It's hard to say goodbye to you but I know that you were brought to me for specific purpose.

Bye …

JEAN ANN: I only wanted to be with him. I float. I'm not certain which nation's shore it is where I wash up when. I am ruined by then, I have wrecked on the shoals, but I can see everything very, very clearly.

JAY: The day I saw something preternatural in the stream.

BEN: And I was so scare and try to run away.

TORY: Memories of the times when gods were men. When there was no such thing as a landowner. We were there and never there. And we remember, and some time in the future our true origins will be read by all, in the invisible histories we maimed and crippled our bodies to plant.

SARAH: Here in these fields, in the firmament, each year.

SONG: LETTING GO (CONTEMPLATION OF THE CURRENTS)

Letting go
Letting go
Letting go of our bodies
Bodies of water
Letting go
Letting go
Letting go

Now I am here and I can contemplate currents
In the fields the kitchen brother into the currents
Shoes didn't come off into the currents
My skirt is wet into the currents
Pink sky water into the currents
Mother waters into the currents
You are not afraid into the currents
From our bodies into the currents
Legs are coming into the currents

Diving flying into the currents
LETTING GO

Light are going down.

There is a visitation of Susan Sontag.

Lights go out.

The End.

MUSIC

composed by Ashley Turba

lyrics by Sibyl Kempson and Ashley Turba

This score premiered at Abrons Arts Center, along with an overture arranged by Gavin Price, by the following players:

Gavin Price	piano, banjo, trombone
Johnny Gasper	clarinet in Bb
Ellery Royston	harp
Robert M. Johanson	guitar
Becca Blackwell	additional guitar

NO LITTLE HOUSE ON SOME PRAIRIE

A rousing anthem sung by Sarah and backed by the cast, using found instruments like those in a parade

10
B
A
A
E
D
D/E
prair - ie, No Lit-tle House on some prair - ie!
3.We did n't set tle this land.
Ah
Ah
14
A
E
D
D/E
A
E
D
D/E
But we work it with our own hands.
You look a-round where you stand.
It's real
Ah
Ah
Ah - Ah - Ah!
18
B
A
A
A7
A6
A
rough, it's been tough, An-n - d.
I go
Hey! Hey! He - y This ain't no
[........Choose your own adventure for this lyric line.....
Ah- ah

22
B
A
A
prair - ie, No Lit-tle House up some prair - ie! I go Hey! Hey!
[Back to unison]
a capella with claps to fir
25
He - y This ain't no prair - ie, No Lit-tle House up some prair - ie!

A SONG OF TRYING TO REMEMBER

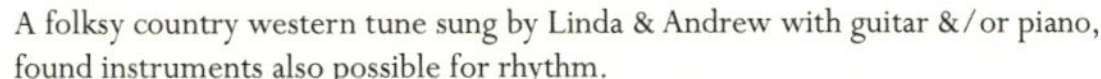
A folksy country western tune sung by Linda & Andrew with guitar &/or piano, found instruments also possible for rhythm.

♩=200

guitar &/or piano

C F G C

6 C F G C

Linda: You were my son, Or I was in Las Veg - as

10 C F G C

We did we en - joy The life of pret - ty dan - ger

14 C F G C

I just can't can - not I can - not re - mem - ber

18 C F G C
inda & ndrew:
Don't piss me off I don't want to go deep - er
22 C F G C
Entire cast sings:
This is a song of try - ing to re - mem - ber
26 C F G C
Day one of pain ex - quis - ite pain with ou - t you
30 C F G C C
I lay face down. un - der the weep - ing wil - low Good - bye Good

35 F G C Bm G
by - e I def-in-ite-ly al-read-y___ told you Why did you have to -
40 Bm G G Bm G Bm G
show up there in per- son. Need - less to say I was o - ver joyed to see you
46 C F G C
This is a song of try-ing to re - mem-ber Though I only remember The
Try a capella
52 C F G C
first two rif - le shots This is a song of try-ing to re - mem-ber

58
C
F
G
C
Good - bye Good - by - e I def - in - ite - ly al - read - y told you
62
C
F
G
C C G C
This is a song of try - ing to re - mem - ber

FOLLIES

A Jazz tune with piano, bass, and clarinet featured sung by Jean Ann, with Sarah harmonizing

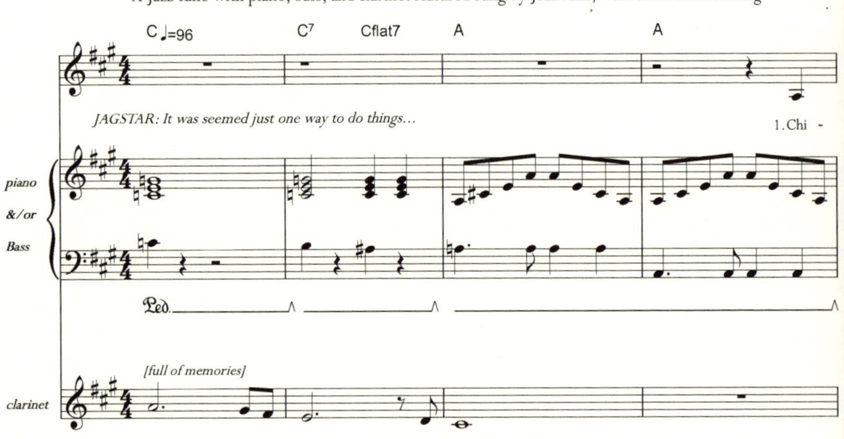

8
E
C
C7
Cflat7
A
Buf - fa - lo. And I, - Well I, for - get some too.
Saint An - tone, And I, Well I, for - get some too.
Ped.
12
A
A7
Ca - 3. These are just some_ of the
Ped.
14
E
A7
E
3
pla - ces we know, Where you can join, The Fol - lies._ Some - bo - dy's

17
C
C7
Cflat7
A
fol - lies, some - bod - y or oth - er trav el in a mot - or coach. And for
21
C
C7
Cflat7
A
3
get everything else, in your ho - tel room.
A A D D
Ped.
tr
26
E E
One of these days, I'm gon - na be
Cof - fee and smokes, lay - in in
I'll go real quiet, and my name could
I could be fierce, and talk with my
E
E
(tempo up to 144) quick & swift of foot,
hushed secrets between the girls

29
E7
E
E
Em
D
Repeat x 4
French I'm tel - ling you French kis - ses, French fries, French bread!
bed I'm tel - ling you put som - ma that old time tunes! and
be I'm tel - ling you my na - me could be Clar - a! and
mouth I'm tel - ling you mouth full of pag - es of books! and
Repeat x 4
32
E
E
E
E7
D
E
D
keep a glass pot of a - pri - cot of ap - ri - cot jam on my bed tray!
37
C
C7
A
A
Ped.
Ped.

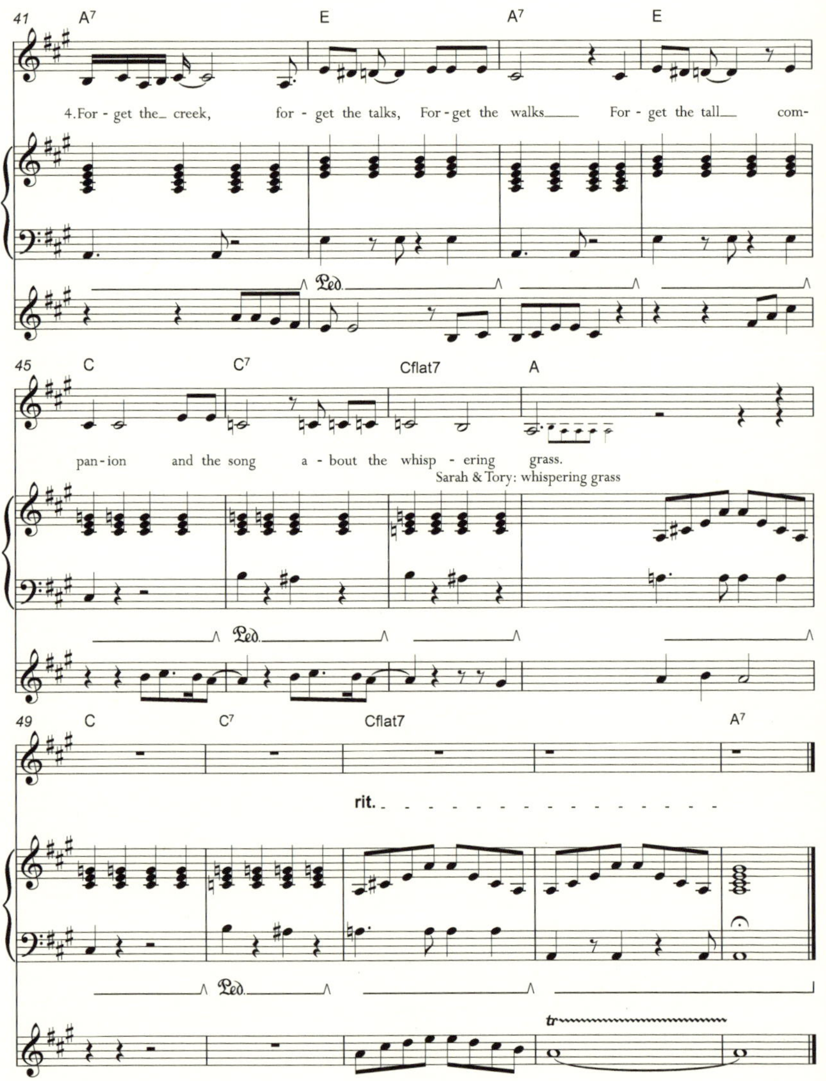
41
A7
E
A7
E
4.For - get the_ creek, for - get the talks, For-get the walks___ For - get the tall___ com-
Ped.
45
C
C7
Cflat7
A
pan-ion and the song a - bout the whisp - ering grass.
Sarah & Tory: whispering grass
Ped.
49
C
C7
Cflat7
A7
rit.
Ped.
tr

TORCH DESIGNS

13
Am
Am
Gm
Gm
Torch de - signs. The thing is just that you can do gas weld-ing
17
Gm
Gm
F
You can do ox - y - gen cut-ting Right now it's the thing I'm
21
most a - bout. Right now it's the thing I'm

25
Hel - lo!
Hel - lo.
thinking most a - bout.
29 Am
Am
Am
Am
2. But you need to have the right tools.
Pur - chase them with
33 Gm
Gm
Gm
mon - ey,
Bar - ter them with
some - thing,
Bor - row them be

37
Am
care - ful.
Tor - ches, blow - pipes, mix - ers, tips.
42
Am
Tor - ches, blow - pipes, mix - ers, tips.
Hel - lo!
Hel - lo.
47
3.Torch
seam
weld,
ac - et - yl ene
Heat
-
ing
valve,
con - nect - tion nut

51
Torch, rear end and nip-ple hose nut con - nect - tion nut
55
See what I mean it's sex - y!
You
60
Am
Hel - lo! Hel - lo. 4.Butt weld
gotta ad - mit it's sex - y

66 Am
Am
Am
Gm
flash weld pro - ject - ion we - ld. It for- ces, re-
70 Gm
Gm
sis tence, push up pres - - - - sure.
74 Am
Am
See what I mean it's sex - y! You got-ta ad - mit it's

79
Am
sex - y!
Hel - lo!
Hel - lo.
5.Con - trol
de -
84
Am
Am
Gm
sign,
high pro - duc - tion
speeds, Nug -
get
size
the trig - ger tip
88
Gm
Gm
Am
Up - set
the
butt
weld - ing,
Grip
the
but - ted
pie - ces,
See
what
I
mean
it's
See what I mean it's

93
Am
sex - y!
[ad lib rocker screams]
You gotta ad - mit it's sex - y!
[Chorus returns, ethereal]
Oooo - ooo - Aaa -
sex - y!
98
Hel - lo! Hel - lo. Hel - lo.
a - - a - - - a - - - ah.
gliss.
gliss.

FOLLIES (REPRISE)

12
A
A7
son.
Cin - cin - at - i -
14
E
A7
E
3
Mil - a -wauk ee Where you can join, Some bo - dy's Fol - lies.__ Cliff
17
C
C7
Cflat7
A
A
Ham - dies, Sil - as Green, or Charles - ton Chew - ey's. And for
21
C
C7
Cflat7
A7
3
get everything else, in your ho - tel room.

25
A
A
A
Transition directly into "Little Pickles"
A
Ben: This I observe... I observe them...
A
29
D
F7
E
C7
A♭(add4)
33
F
F
F
1.Now I am here and I can
Start of "Little Pickles"
Ped.

LITTLE PICKLES

10
Eb
Gm
F
F
hus - band sis - ter friend. Wash the sup - per dish - es so
Ped.
12
Eb
Gm
F
[Men only:]
F
greas - y from the pork. [While we smoke out on the
Ped.
14
Gm
F Gm F
Gm
porch.]
Jean Ann: Oh those lit-tle pick - les!
Fa - ncy stained glass win - dow spoons

25
Hel - lo!
Hel - lo.
thinking most a - bout.
29 Am
Am
Am
Am
2. But you need to have the right tools.
Pur - chase them with
33 Gm
Gm
Gm
mon - ey,
Bar - ter them with some - thing,
Bor - row them be

37
Am
care - ful.
Tor - ches, blow - pipes, mix - ers, tips.
42
Am
Hel - lo!
Hel - lo.
Tor - ches, blow - pipes, mix - ers, tips.
47
3. Torch seam weld, ac - et - yl ene Heat - ing valve, con - nect - tion nut

37
F
Gm
F
These old vague mis shap - en pick les I could throw them a - cross the room til af - ter our
40
E♭
Gm
E♭
F
ev - er aft - er I'll ne - ver get - a lit - tle pick - le a - gain.
Ped.
44
E♭
[Humming/riffing...]
Ped.
F

47
Gm
F
Ped.

PERSON TO PERSON

Fm
[Andrew speaks, flute plays melody:]
of.
Head.
1. He holds her fixed distance away, fixed then not too far away. They are safe.
2. He walks next to her. They climb on the rocks. She knows and begins to know ringing…
[Tory speaks:]
2. …Ringing reaches upward. He is one person. She is one person.
2. Andrew. Cut. The shit.
Fm
Gm
Gm
3.I
Love,
My
Fm
Fm
Love - - .
Ah uh uh
Ah uh uh [whistling
whistling]

BLACK BLACK SLEEP

26
black, sleep. A black, black, sleep. A black,
black, - - sleep - .

L'IMAGE

Suspenseful chamber piece; piano can be substituted for guitars.

7
F
F
1. they are full of some strange passione étrangée and hidden meaning - oh! Ah! They speak to me alone!
1.L'im
2.L'im
9
Am
Am
Am
a - ge. On voie en
a - ge. Les bêtes les
12
C
Dm
vue on joue dans
larmes des en fants

14 G
Am
Am
les soir - ées.
Les
mes for - tées.
Mes
17 Am
Am
Dm
Am
soi - ré - e - s!
L'im - a - ge!
for - té - e - s!
L'im - a - ge!
20 Am
Am
Am
3. Plus also plus the Formal Relationship -

23
Am Bm C G F C
Un Loup un rou-ga-rou- Le Pomp-i-
gliss.
gliss.
26
Dm Am F
dou loup ga-rou. Un Loup un rou-ga
F
gliss.
gliss.
gliss.
29
C Dm Am
rou Le Pomp-i-dou loup - ga -rou.
gliss.
gliss.
gliss.

32
Am
Am
Am
L'i - ma - - - - - -

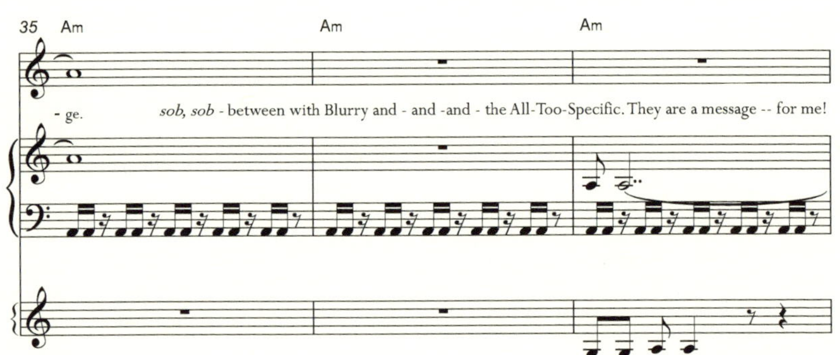
35
Am
Am
Am
- ge.
sob, sob - between with Blurry and - and -and - the All-Too-Specific. They are a message -- for me!

38
Am
Am Em
Em
I am overcome...
One moment please... [he gestures to orchestra to stop]

[He drops to his knees. He weeps into his hankerchief until it is sopping wet. He whimpers.]
It's too much - it's too MUCH! Ah, GOD! What does it MEAN I DON'T KNOW WHAT IT MEANS!!
I feel I can almost recognize in these an order of deep visual meaning which I receive only by divine universal providence.
41
Am
Am
44
F
F
L'eau -
46
Am
Am
ciel
L'eau -
ciel
L'eau
48
Dm
F
Am
ciel
L'eau -
ciel
L'eau -
ciel.

YELLOW SHOES

A Scott Joplin-type rag, can be sung with found instruments among the cast, such as washboard. Sung by Susan Sontag, Jay, Ben, and cast.

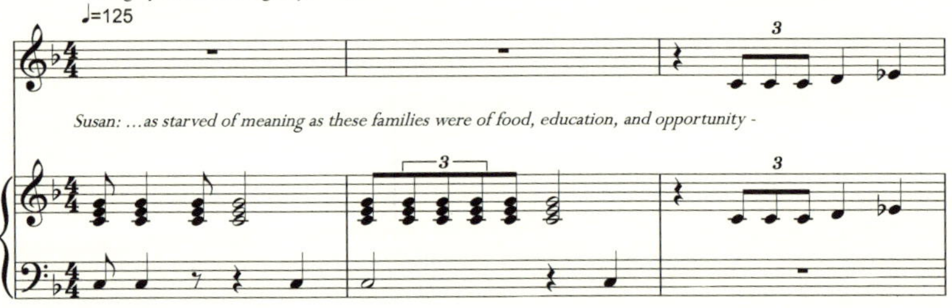

11
C C C
Ben&Jay: Their suf-fer-ing was real - ly real What were the terms of our
3
15
C C C F
ap- peal? We onl - y told what we could name, 'n' what we still feel.
19
F Dm F
Susan: So say good bye to blame-less-ness Buh-bye to mor-al de-cenc-y
3
Ped.
23
Dm F
Ben&Jay: For all our prec - ious pho - to - graph - ic
Ped.

25 Dm
F
ev - i - dence,_ In the end we chose not to see!
27 Dm
stridently...
31
Ben&Jay: Re gard-ing
36 C
C
C
F
the mult - i- tudes in dis - re- gard One can't ap- peal to what's

39
C
C
C
— ac - quired
Susan: Their pain could speak, but they_
41
[cast joins in singing:]
F
— were weak Susan: They were just too tired.
Cast: We were just too tired.
3
Susan: You
Cast: You
44
F
Dm
F
left their hearts just big emp - ty holes They knew no rest un - til they died.
left our hearts just big emp - ty holes we knew no rest un - til we died.
Ped.
47
Dm
F
Dm
F
Ben&Jay: What we learned lay in what we stole Con-cealed cause caused our lies.
Ped.
Ped.

51
Dm
stridently...
Ped.
Ped.
55
Ped.

A SONG OF TRYING TO REMEMBER (REPRISE)

A folksy country western tune sung reprised by Linda & Andrew with guitar &/or piano, found instruments also possible for rhythm. Jean Ann adds ad lib flourishes & echoes.

14
C
F
G
C C G C
grand - sons hum this song, call it 'See You In Sept - em - ber'?
grand - sons hum this so - ng, call it 'See You In Sept - em - ber'?

LETTING GO

Allegro
hoir
Let - ting Go - - .
Allegro
Em D A D A Em D A D A
iano
7
Let - ting Go - - . Let - ting Go - of-the wa-a-ters, deep clear
Em D A D A Em D A G
13
wa - ters. Let-ting go of the bo-d-ies bo-dies of wa -
G D A G D

18
ter. Let-ting go. Let - ting go - - Let - ting go -
C A F Em A A F Em A
24
A A
- Now I am here and I can cont-em-plate cur-rents In the fields the kitch-en bro-ther
C D A
28
in-to the cur - rents 1.shoes didn't come off in-to the cur - rents 1.my skirt is wet
2.you are not afraid! 2.From our bod-ies
C D A C D A

32
in-to the cur - rents 1.pink sky water in-to the cur - rents 1.mo ther wa - ters
2.Legs are com-i-ng 2.Div - ing fly- ing
C D A C D A
36
in - to the cur - rents LET - -
C D A C
39
- - TING - - - - go.
D D

BIBLIOGRAPHY

Agee, James and Walker Evans. *Cotton Tenants*. Brooklyn, NY: Melville House Publishing, 2013.

Agee, James and Walker Evans. *Let Us Now Praise Famous Men*. New York: Houghton Mifflin, 1939.

Barthes, Roland. *Camera Lucida*. New York: Hill and Wang, 1980.

Cather, Willa. *O Pioneers!* Mineola, NY: Dover Thrift Editions, 1993.

Conrad, Joseph. Author's Note. *The Shadow Line*. By Conrad. London: J.M. Dent & Sons, Ltd., 1920.

Eisenman, Stephen F. *The Abu Ghraib Effect*. London: Reaktion Books, 2007.

Redon, Odilon. *To Myself: Notes on Life, Art, and Artists*. Trans. Mira Jacob and Jeanne L. Wasserman. New York: George Braziller, Inc., 1986.

Sauer, Carl. *Land and Life*. Ed. John Leighly. Berkeley: University of California Press, 1969.

Sontag, Susan. *On Photography*. New York: Picador, 1973.

REFERENCES

"Whaddya think my name is Fink and I press pants for nothing!" (p.20)

Refers to an old Yiddish punctuation joke.

"I'm talking about this circle of pillars..." (p.21)

Refers to the short story by Jorge Luis Borges, "The Circular Ruins."

"Kilt-wearing bearded hero fights against big cats ..." (p.21)

What Tory arrives at here is a list that she continues and perpetuates throughout the play. In terms of the writing, it is taken directly from a curatorial moniker describing a such scene from one of the collected Assyrian cylinder seals in the J.P. Morgan collection at the Morgan Library in NYC.

In our production, these almost hilariously pedestrian descriptions were treated as "visions" of some kind: images from a temporal dimension running parallel to hers/theirs/ours in the geography, that poke through into the time and place of the play and performance, using Tory's imaginative consciousness as a conduit.

"A whole full outfit..." (p.22)

This story is from a young adult's novel I read in adolescence, but I can't remember the name of it. It was about an adolescent girl who grew up on the wrong side of the tracks. To make up for some unfairness of vaguely tragic proportions (it was a particular event that pronounced itself beyond the quotidian landscape of her low birth) that had befallen her, a woman-of-standing in the town gifted her an outfit of clothing, and left it at that. The outfit in that story met a similar fate of gradual decomposition as the one shown and described here.

"TENANT FARMERS DO NOT PLOW IN SWALLOWTAILS..." (p.23)

This is a direct quote from *Cotton Tenants* by James Agee, an unpublished typescript containing the actual article that was submitted to *Fortune* magazine and subsequently rejected. It had only recently been found among Agee's belongings when this play was written. The saying was apparently a common one of the day.

"a grass lawn on it made out of real green ribbon." (p.24)

In 1997 I made a set of 'craft vests' as costumes for Richard Maxwell's play *Flight Courier Service*. They were reversible and holiday-themed. I was, and remain, particularly fond and proud of the "Easter" vest, on which I planted an actual green lawn of green ribbon, littered with partially-hidden Easter eggs. This play was begun as a commission for the Playwrights' Division of New York City Players, so these introductory sections contain various references and shout-outs to other plays in the NYCP cannon. This is one of them, with a personal connection.

"a fair in the basement ... a dozen or so lovelorn attitudes." (p.27)

This scenario and others of this section are borrowed from Willa Cather's novel *O Pioneers!*

"You don't remember me, Linda?" (p.33)

Another remnant of the cancelled NYCP commissioning, that didn't feel right to cut out, not slightly becayse of the proliferating connections encircling it. *Vision Disturbance* is a play by Christina Masciotti that was commissioned by the Playwrights Division of NYCP. In the original production in the Playhouse at Abrons Arts Center, Linda Mancini played a woman with a particular ocular ailment that is treated by Jay Smith's character. The two form a relationship. At one time, Kate Valk told her friend Tanya Selvaratnam that there were two playwrights she should meet: Christina Masciotti and myself. Tanya had coffee with Christina and told her about a certain ocular ailment from which she was healing, which later became the subject of *Vision Disturbance*. I also had the recommended coffee with Tanya and still later, I unwittingly cast her in the role I had originally written for Linda. (It had been my intention to create a sort of echo chamber of past NYCP productions by casting a lot of the same actors and referring to a lot of the same moments in these other plays.) And so a strange circle of events, references, and referrals was formed.

"You look familiar to me too" (p.33)

This recollection of Linda's refers to Ben Williams' character in *Dreamless Land* by Julia Jarcho, which premiered in the Underground Theater at Abrons Arts Center. In keeping with the same echo chamber idea, I had originally intended to cast Ben as Ben in direct reference to Julia's play, which had also been an NYCP production.

"This is a song of trying to remember." (p.34)

Here Linda is recalling another reality that she lived in the past, which is her alternate life in *Dreamless Land* where Linda Mancini played, among other characters or versions of one character, a Las Vegas showgirl. Linda also recalls a scene from *O Pioneers!* when a pair of star-crossed adulterous lovers are caught and murdered by the cuckolded husband.

"Seated Man With Unshaved Neck ..." (p.38)

The descriptions that begin to occur through Sarah in this and succeeding scenes mirror the basic syntactical set-up of Tory's "visions," but with different content that pulls rather from the immediate and far-reaching future than the distant past: that of the photographs themselves. Hers are an alchemy of their own current predicament taken from inside Jay's future self.

From Mircea Eliade's *Patterns in Comparative Religion* I learned that narratives become our mythology by their repeated use, our amalgamated recognition over time. Images are carved by human beings in stone or crystal or are conjured in a chemical soak to celluloid that reveals the presences and absences of light in a single instant. A vast variety of materials holds the record of it, of our mythology. Depending on their form and how close they remain to (or how far they have been removed from) their natural version, they hold it because they are bidden to but also unbeknownst to us (unless we are looking very closely with an ancient quality of attention), irrespectively. The rings on the trees, the reach of the energy in their limbs, their re-composition into thin tissue typewriter paper that withstands and then holds the stamp of the typewriter keys as an imprint, a scar. Or the knife in the bark, marking – with its labor-intensive confession – the loss of virginity, the shedding of tears. How the dignity or awkwardness of the method of recording determines, over time, the bearing the depicted content will have on our collected imaginative consciousness. Is the mythology affected by the quality of the material used to keep and tell it? Later, in his darkroom (in an earlier draft), Jay would say to Sarah's image on the 8x10 something like, "perhaps if I had etched you, you would not now be so inferior" – an idea that belonged to Odilon Redon, and which I felt expressed aptly the above sentiments, but was too much verbiage for the theatrical moment at hand.

Machines (p.46)

The machine stuff is largely from *The New American Machinists Handbook*.

"Large Mass of Half Cloud Half Sandy Beach ..." (p.55)

At this point in the progression of images it seemed fitting to open Tory's intake valve to another aesthetic influence. What she delivers here is a description of Odilon Redon's Adapa – which I stumbled across early on in my research and which dumbfounded me with its luminous strangeness. Only later did I discover the likeness in content between it and the cuneiform tablet fragments displayed in the Morgan Library right alongside the collected cylinder seals referenced in Tory's other visions. Carl Sagan, I.S. Shklovski and John Lash have all linked the myth of Adapa/Oannes to the paleocontact hypothesis: a claim that intelligent extraterrestrial beings may have visited the Earth in ancient times and profoundly affected the development of human civilization. Petro-, heiro- and geo-glyphic evidence worldwide are used by the theory's proponents to support the hypothesis.

I was attracted to the mutually exclusive relationship between knowledge and immortality inherent in the story of Adapa/Oannes – another, more feminine version of Adam, because of his fishiness, his unwittingly anti-heroic dismissal of immortality in favor of knowledge (which I went ahead and connected to the land and its now oft-ignored cycles of fertility). I was then struck and very taken with a connection Jody McAuliffe made between the alleged goings-on of that long-ago Sumerian/Mesopotamian/Assyrian period (mentioned above), and the endeavors of the Moundbuilders of the Mississippian period who were active on the same Alabama land that these tenant farmers worked, during a time when glyphs and oral history were the main modes of record-keeping.

It was Jody also who alerted me to Stephen Eiseman's *The Abu Graib Effect,* which holds those photographs of the torture and mistreatment of Islamic prisoners (about which Susan Sontag also wrote in her 2004 New York Times essay "Regarding the Torture of Others") to the same "pathos formula" as works of Michelangelo, and of imperial Greek and Roman art in which images of political subjugation and atrocity are pushed into the same realm of "passionate suffering" that Sontag suggests in On Photography. Again, by igniting our response of aesthetic appreciation, our impulse to active public opposition is quelled.

Since 2013 when I began working on this play in earnest at Duke University, the demolition of ancient works of Assyrian art has been perpetrated in Mosul, Nimrud, Hatra, Ninevah, and other cities. Suddenly the images Tory describes in her visions took on a new resonance, the deterioration of their meaning in our memory is accelerated along with the loss of their physical existence and ontology.

With time, these circles of connection in 'random' and intuitively-guided research almost always reveal a deeper order at work that a conscious, logical, discursive frame of inquiry will too-easily dismiss or even fail altogether to recognize altogether. These connective circles do not adhere to the timeclock of a downtown production schedule, however, and their full implications are still unfolding and revealing themselves in the wake of the show's run.

"In this world of nature..." (p.62)

From *To Myself: Notes on Life, Art, and Artists* by Odilon Redon.

LET US NOW PRAISE SUSAN SONTAG was developed at Duke University, Sarah Lawrence College, and New Dramatists. At the moment of this publication, it will have premiered in the Underground Theater at the Abrons Arts Center on Grand Street in New York City, as the inaugural production of the 7 Daughters of Eve Thtr. & Perf. Co., under Sibyl Kempson's direction, with staging and choreography by David Neumann, music by Ashley Turba, musical direction by Gavin Price, dramaturgy by Jody McAuliffe and and Eryk Aughenbaugh, set and costume design by Suzanne Bocanegra, with construction help from Brendan Regimbal, Laurena Allan and Jake Denney, lighting design by Sarah Lurie, stage management by Eryk Aughenbaugh and Tavish Miller, and understudying by Tavish Miller. The production was made possible by generous support from the Jerome Foundation and Abrons Arts Center.

Thanks to Jody McAuliffe, Eleanor Savage, David Neumann, Ashley Turba, Miriam Sauls, Christine Farrell, Emily Morse, John Steber, Joel Ruark, Elena Heyman, Karinne Keithley, Jay Wegman, Richard Maxwell, Lindsay Hockaday, Antje Oegel, Casey Llewellyn, Tei Blow, Oceana James, Meg Zinky, Molly Zimmelman, Daphne Gaines, Cindy Cheung, Jack Frederick, A.P. Andrews, Eryk Aughenbaugh, Sarah Willis, Lauren Reinhard, Emily Ritger, Stephen Tyler Davis, Noelle Clark, Megan Gilbert, Wendy Schibener, Liza Truschel, Alyssa Sprague, Gabrielle Schutz, Allison Snyder, Michelle Hernandez, Chris Aldrich, Jack Sullivan, Collin Bradley, Jesse Koehler, Elena Lagon, Faye Goodwin, Tierney Marey, Rachel Freedman, Madeleine Pron, Mike Myers, Carl Martin, Cullen Burling, Daisygreen Stenhouse, and Thomas Kavanagh.

Sibyl Kempson's plays have been presented in the United States, Germany, and Norway. She lives in New York City and the Pocono Mountains of Pennsylvania, and has founded the 7 Daughters of Eve Thtr. & Perf. Co., of which the premiere of LET US NOW PRAISE SUSAN SONTAG at Abrons Arts Center in NYC is the inaugural production. She is a resident playwright at New Dramatists, a 2014 USA Artists Rockefeller Fellow, a MacDowell Colony Fellow, and an Artist-in-Residence at Abrons Arts Center. She has an MFA from Brooklyn College and teaches playwriting at Sarah Lawrence College.

53rd State Press publishes new writing for performance, interdisciplinary performance documentation, and dance pamphlets. It was founded in 2007 and is coedited by Antje Oegel and Karinne Keithley Syers. For more information or to subscribe, please visit 53rdstatepress.org.

53rd State Press books are represented by Theatre Communications Group, and distributed to the book trade by Consortium Book Distribution. Please contact Consortium directly for trade orders.

This book was designed by Casey Llewellyn and Karinne Keithley Syers.

Front and Back Cover photographs by Peter Serling, showing Suzanne Bocanegra's costumes for Sarah Willis (front) and Tanya Selvaratnam (back).

1 The Book of the Dog//Karinne Keithley

2 Joyce Cho Plays//Joyce Cho

3 No Dice//Nature Theater of Oklahoma

4 Rambo Solo//Nature Theater of Oklahoma

5 When You Rise Up//Miguel Gutierrez

6 Montgomery Park, or Opulence//Karinne Keithley

7 Crime or Emergency//Sibyl Kempson

8 Off the Hozzle//Rob Erickson

9 A Map of Virtue and Black Cat Lost//Erin Courtney

10 Pig Iron: Three Plays//Pig Iron Theatre Company

11 The Mayor of Baltimore and Anthem//Kristen Kosmas

12 Ich, KürbisGeist and The Secret Death of Puppets//Sibyl Kempson

13 Soulographie: Our Genocides//Erik Ehn

14 Life and Times: Episode 1//Nature Theater of Oklahoma

15 Life and Times: Episode 2//Nature Theater of Oklahoma

16 Life and Times: Episodes 3 &4//Nature Theater of Oklahoma

17 The 53rd State Occasional No. 1//Ed. Paul Lazar

18 Seagull (Thinking of you)//Tina Satter

19 There There//Kristen Kosmas

20 Another Telepathic Thing//Big Dance Theater

21 Another Tree Dance//Karinne Keithley Syers

22 Let Us Now Praise Susan Sontag//Sibyl Kempson

Dance Pamphlet No. 1: Self Made Man Man Made Land//Ursula Eagly

Dance Pamphlet No. 2: Dance by Letter//Annie-B Parson